Abingdon's Intergenerational Programs

Naomi Mitchum

Abingdon Press

Abingdon's Intergenerational Programs

Naomi Mitchum

Abingdon Press

Abingdon's Intergenerational Programs

Copyright © 1991 by Abingdon Press

Abingdon Press hereby grants permission to local churches to reproduce the material contained in this publication for purposes of rehearsal and performance, provided the following notice appears on each copy: From *Abingdon's Intergenerational Programs* Copyright © 1991 by Abingdon Press. No further reproduction or distribution of this material is allowed without the written consent of Abingdon Press, 201 Eighth Avenue South, Nashville, TN 37202.

This book is printed on acid-free paper.

ISBN 0-687-00474-8

All Scripture quotations are from The New International Version, New Testament. Copyright © 1973 by The New York Bible Society International. Used by permission.

MANUFACTURED IN THE UNITED STATES OF AMERICA

CONTENTS

INTRODUCTION

THE WHY AND HOW
OF INTERGENERATIONAL DRAMA EVENTS

Abingdon's Intergenerational Programs reflects the challenges of a fragmented society in which life-styles have changed and family units have undergone drastic redefinitions. The dramas in this book are designed to call attention to these challenges and to common issues important to persons of all ages. The dramas have been embroidered with related activities that form a vehicle for interaction between persons so they may communicate through play, projects, worship, idea exchange, and the Heart Family adoption plan. Thus, rather than assemble to talk about intergenerational differences as so many programs do, *Abingdon's Intergenerational Programs* is designed to provide for experiences shared by persons of different age levels.

Planned intergenerational events that engage persons of two or more generations in face-to-face interaction can never take the place of the inter-age unplanned experiences that enrich the life of a congregation, such as weddings, baptisms, passing greetings in the corridors, or nods of affirmation upon entering a meeting or worship service. The planned events can, however, help persons of all ages hold hands as they explore common threads of interest and say to each other, "You are important."

A congregation's intergenerational task is broadly defined in the ritual promise it makes to a person being baptized in The United Methodist Church:

> *With God's help we will so order our lives after the example of Christ that,* surrounded by steadfast love, *you may be established in the faith, and confirmed and strengthened in the way that leads to life eternal.*

The pledge to surround a person with steadfast love suggests that we are called to new relationships with each other and with God. We are called to be in community as children of God. We are called to be members one of another (Eph. 4:24). We are called to affirm and learn from one another, and we are called to enjoy each other!

WHY USE DRAMA?

The church by its nature is inclusive, but sometimes we unknowingly erect barriers because of age, intellectual prowess, education, race, or handicapping conditions. Drama is a tool the church can use to draw diverse people together. This is possible because drama can be an activity that focuses ideas and dares to explore issues not yet put into words. It is specific, bringing ideas from the abstract of way-out-there-somewhere to the here-and-now with real people speaking real words about life. One of drama's greatest assets is that it presents layers of thought! In a single playlet, children may see a simple story; youth may find clues to their identities and gain new insights; adults may experience intellectual and spiritual challenges, and find ways to appropriate faith into life. During drama related activities, persons of all ages strip away unessentials and get right to the bones of an issue. They may share experiences and viewpoints, ask each other important questions, and help each other with answers.

HOW TO USE THIS BOOK

Forms of drama presented in *Abingdon's Intergenerational Programs* include playlets, skits, a play, tableaux, a puppet show, reader's theater, dramatic singing, dramatic reading, monologues, and dialogues. All are meant to be easily prepared. Some will work best with memorized character parts, stage props, and costumes. However, you may wish to use skits and playlets as read-throughs where actors rehearse stage movements, practice reading, and present the drama with scripts in their hands. If stage sets are a problem, the moderator or narrator may describe in detail an imaginary setting or simply tell the setting, such as, "The setting is the bank of a river," or, "Our characters are in the kitchen at dinner time."

Although they are educational, issue oriented, and focusing agents, the dramas in this book are meant to be fun! That's f-u-n! Bend the dialogue, transplant parts, add local comedy, cast parts with incongruity. Hang a sign around a ten-year-old's neck saying "grandma" and cast grandma as a seven-year-old. When it seems appropriate, use the three main elements of humor: exaggeration, incongruity, and absurdity.

DIVIDE OWNERSHIP OF YOUR DRAMA EVENT

Each drama in this book has been developed in detail to provide handy guidelines for planning. But there is a danger in writing a book that encompasses full-blown plans for events. The event plans are not quick-fix programs entered into lightly at the last minute. Each person or committee selecting a drama event must consider the needs and interests of the local congregation and adapt the plans accordingly. Seek help! Encourage input by representatives of various age groups. Make the events theirs.

Decide on the vehicle for helping meet congregational needs. Will it be a weekend retreat, an evening or daylong event, or series of events? Will it be a campout of parents and teenagers or on all-day sharing of children with their grandparents? Will it be parents and children making things together? Will it be a family night including Heart Families? (Heart Family is an adoption program for pairing single children, youth, or adults with a family unit. A family unit may be one or more persons.) All these age mixes may be considered intergenerational if the event involves two or more generations *grouped together*. It doesn't count as intergenerational if the age groups are meeting separately at the same time, as no idea sharing takes place and no personal relationships develop.

THE MODERATOR'S TASK

The moderator ties each event together with a mix of skillful direction, flexibility, and humor. The moderator's actions imply, "I'm in charge right now, but it's your event." As groups are forming, they need the comfort of knowing that something is planned and it has direction; the moderator provides that direction. The event's opening minutes may foretell the success or failure of accomplishing the goals you have set. The moderator's "inchargeness," the greeters and persons who assist with nametags, and those responsible for get together activities all contribute to a beginning that makes persons feel comfortable and at home in an intergenerational event.

INSTRUCTIONS FOR DRAMA LEADERS

Take the task seriously as you plan, but relax and enjoy working and playing with drama volunteers.

1. Read the drama until you understand its focus and the qualities of each character. Change language to fit your local setting. Visualize the actors on your staging area. Imagine how and where they will move. Seeing the actors on stage in your mind's eye is the first step in blocking a skit or play. Blocking is your part in telling the actors what to do and where to do it.

2. Make script copies.

3. Recruit actors and necessary staging help.

4. Provide highlighters or marking pens, and instruct each actor to highlight his or her dialogue and stage directions.

5. Rehearse with props in place, if possible. If not, use stand-in props of similar size.

6. Expect lines to be memorized by the third rehearsal. (Option: Many groups use a read-through as a final presentation. Rehearsals are still mandatory. In the case of reader's theater and dramatic reading presentations, rehearsals must be on location, as acoustics vary.)

7. After the production, congratulate and applaud actors and crew.

8. Return all props and file script copies for future use.

ADDITIONAL TIPS FOR MONOLOGUE DIRECTION

A monologue actor must establish eye contact with the object of his or her dialogue. For example, St. Francis (Peace event) talks to and looks at the imaginary Bernard who sits across the table from him. However, in "Handicapped to Cheeseburger" (It's All Right to Be Different event), Jeff Martin is talking to the audience, and should establish eye contact with them. Pauses, as noted in the script, and physical activity hold the audience's interest.

STAGING

Stage directions are based on common theater usage. Early stages were built with the rear of the stage elevated for better viewing. For that reason, the rear of the stage is called *upstage,* and the area of stage nearest the audience is called *downstage.* Other directions assume that one is facing the audience. *Stage left,* therefore, is to the left of an onstage actor, and *stage right* is to the right of an actor.

THE DISCUSSION LEADER'S TASK

Group discussion is a powerful learning tool that can only succeed in an environment of acceptance. If persons of all ages feel they will be accepted as persons and that their conversation will be taken as sincere expressions of themselves, they will respond readily. Help a group bond by using time to establish each person's identity and make him or her feel important. Try a circular response in which everyone shares names and such things as favorite color, food, water sport, type of reading, vacation preference, a description of a perfect Sunday afternoon, what they like on a hot dog, and so forth.

A good leader will work out a pattern he or she hopes the group will follow, but the plan must be flexible. Write key questions on paper, or circle the questions you will use from those suggested after each drama. Prioritize them according to the ages to be represented in your discussion group. Reproduce copies of the prioritized questions for the discussion leaders. There is no one way to lead a discussion, but there are guidelines for developing your own techniques:

1. Know in advance which age levels will be represented in the group.
2. Expect that members of your group will respond. Resist the impulse to jump in quickly with an answer. *There is no one answer.* Discussion is an open consideration where each contribution is important.
3. The discussion question must be clearly stated and must not allow for a yes or no answer.
4. The leader may reflect back an answer and ask why a person thinks as he or she does. Ask for clarification in a positive way. Use this technique only after persons in the group are acquainted and discussion is flowing.
5. Restate a question or comment to clarify it. Examples: "I hear you saying . . ." or "Is this what you are saying . . . ?", or "I think I heard you ask . . . ."
6. Successful intergenerational discussion demands that the leader be constantly alert to domination by one person or age group. Break into long speeches with suggestions like "May we hear a parent's response to that idea?" or "I understand your point of view. Who will give a child's opinion?" or "Well stated. Who has another idea along those lines?" Affirm the dominator, but move on.
7. Clearly state directions if discussion is followed by role play or other activity. Take the first turn in the activity to illustrate your directions. This gives group members time to think and respond, and sends the message that you are sharing yourself.
8. Follow your group's interests, but put a boundary on how far astray the group can go. Interrupt by saying, "This is interesting, but let's hold it for the end of our time together." Restate the original discussion topic. If you have time later, return to the off-topic subject.

Discussion—a give and take of ideas—may be accomplished in buzz groups (sometimes called huddle groups) where subgroups have discussions, then share their thoughts with the larger group. Many arrangements make these interesting: triads (3), duos (2), or back-to-back (2).

EVENT THEME: WE'RE FAMILY

OUR FAMILIES ARE DIFFERENT, BUT WE ARE ALL IN ONE CHURCH FAMILY.

SCHEDULE

*Get nametags.
*Get Together Activities:
  1. Make headbands.
  2. Play games.
  3. Fill out the questionnaire and discuss results.
*Eat a picnic lunch.
*Focus Activities:
  1. Watch skit: *The Ant Who Had Twelve Uncles.*
  2. If you are *not* using *The Ant Who Had Twelve Uncles,* make up skits about church and/or family values.
*Sharing Time:
  1. Discuss families.
  2. Celebrate church family (yeah-yeah time).

ADVANCE PREPARATION

*Recruit a moderator.
*Plan for nametags and get someone to supervise making of headbands.
*Recruit a game leader.
*Select a skit director.
*Make copies of the questionnaire to use in small groups.
*If you are not using the skit, select group leaders who will prepare for family values skit making. Use scripture references under discussion section of this event for ideas. Skits should answer the questions, What value can be most important in families? Does a family value honesty? Integrity? Church attendance? Relationship to God? Expressions of love? Gratitude? Self-discipline?

ROOM ARRANGEMENT

*A table for nametags should be placed near the door.
*There should be a large area for game playing, with chairs available for those who cannot sit on floor.

*In another area, arrange chairs in semicircle around staging area. Block off first row of chairs, stage left, for eleven actors. (Stage left is described as to your left as you stand facing the audience.)

AS PEOPLE ARRIVE

*Get the nametags.
*Inaugurate a Heart Family adoption program for pairing children and youth with single adults or a couple. Or help a parent(s)-and-children family adopt an aunt, uncle, grandmother, grandfather, or another child. Prepare paper, staples, crayons or marking pens, glitter and glue for making headbands for Heart-Family units.
*Begin the games.

GAMES

Clothespins

Supplies needed: Two snap clothespins for each person. At the nametag table, pin two snap clothespins on each person.

Instructions: The object is to get rid of the clothespins and keep others from snapping a clothespin on you. Be sneaky. Before beginning relays, announce the winner with the least number of clothespins, and the scapegoat with the most.

Family Cooperation[1]

Supplies needed: Several dozen jar rings and several brooms.

Instructions: work in pairs as people begin to arrive. Each pair takes a turn with one partner holding a broom about ten feet (four for small children) away from the other partner, who throws six jar rings. The partner holding the broom must keep his or her foot on the broom straws, so that the bottom never moves. But he or she can move the handle to catch the jar rings thrown by his partner. After one person throws the rings, the partners then change places. The six rings are left on the handle, and the other person throws six more. The couple with the most rings on the broom wins. This game is like a family. If would be difficult to catch all rings without partners working toward a common goal.

Family Cleanup

Supplies needed: A broom and small aluminum pie tin for each team.

Instructions: Organize the group into relay teams. Each contestant must sweep the pie tin fifteen feet to a tape-marked spot and back.

[1]Adapted from *The Best of Try This One,* Thom Schultz, ed. (Loveland, CO.: Group Books, 1981), p. 43.

Washday Relay[2]

Supplies needed: Scarves, clothespins, and a clothesline—for each team—that is suspended low enough for the smallest contestant. Don't worry if you can't suspend the line; it is even harder to hang clothes on a limp line.

Instructions: The first player of each relay team is given two scarves and three clothespins. At the signal, player number one of each team runs to a clothesline, hangs his or her wash, and returns to the end of the relay line. The next player runs up, takes down the laundry, gives it to the third person in line, who hangs it, and so on to the end of the team. The team finishing first is the winner.

Questionnaires

Supplies: Prepared list of questions.

Instructions: Seat each relay team in a circle. Appoint a leader and give him or her a question sheet. Have each person in the circle take a turn answering the question. If you have young children, shorten the list. Add questions reflecting your emphasis for the event.

Answer the Questions

1. What is your favorite food?
2. Name your brothers or sisters.
3. Families change. How many people are in your family now? How many people were in your family several years ago?
4. Who cleans the dishes at your house?
5. What is your favorite game?
6. What is your family's favorite game?
7. How many times have you moved?
8. Who makes your home secure at night?
9. What is your favorite childhood memory?
10. How much homework (or reading) do you do every day?
11. Who buys the groceries at your house?
12. Who says a prayer at your house?
13. Which family members live a distance from your house?

Option

Play spin the bottle and ask family-type questions. For example: What do you do every day? Did you set the breakfast table today? Do you like to be alone? What is your favorite time of day?

---

[2]*Games for All Ages and How to Use Them,* Marjorie Wackerbarth and Lillian S. Graham (Grand Rapids: Baker Book House, 1980), p. 63.

FOCUS ACTIVITY

THE ANT WHO HAD TWELVE UNCLES
A skit about all kinds of families.

Production Notes

Characters: The following characters have scripted parts: Moderator, Antron (a male Leafcutter ant), Antrix (a female Harvester ant), Anteleven (a male Leafcutter ant), and the following male ants: Uncle Scott, Uncle Jeff, Uncle Jeremiah, Uncle Lewis, Uncle Robert, Uncle Paul, Uncle Al, and Uncle Bill.

The following characters sit in the audience wearing ant head antennae: Uncle Bud, Uncle David, Uncle Philip, Uncle Ivan, Grandma Maple, Granny Hill, Grandma Hickory, Grandma Chestnut, Granny Oak, Grandma Holly, Granny Cedar, and Great Grandma Magnolia.

Playing Time: 6-10 minutes

Properties: Three wooden cubes of varying sizes, or use small, medium, and large chairs or benches. Antron carries an oversized (one-by-three-foot) piece of celery; Antrix carries a large posterboard chocolate chip cookie with nuts and a sheaf of weeds; Anteleven carries several oversized (two-by-three-foot) leaves and a huge cardboard baked bean. Each uncle carries at least one large leaf. One large leaf is center stage on the floor. Make the leaves from cardboard or use pillows with green or brown covers, anything to give the impression that the ant is carrying something large and heavy.

Costumes: All characters wear head antennae and brown clothing. Antrix wears noticeably large shoes.

Setting: The scene is a forest. A large wooden cube sits stage right. A medium cube is downstage left, and a smaller cube is slightly to the right of the medium cube, and back about three feet. Chairs for the audience have been arranged in a semicircle around the staging area. All ants having scripted parts are seated in the front row of these chairs to stage left. Unscripted uncles and the grandmas, all wearing ant antennae, are seated throughout the audience.

Note to director: This is a slapstick sort of play. A lot of the humor comes from seeing people dressed as ants. Warn actors to allow the audience some laugh time before beginning lines. However, too much laugh time may cause the play to lose its momentum. Rehearse the play in front of a few laughers.

MODERATOR: The church is a place where everyone belongs. People who come to our church love and support each other. We call this church family. Today we welcome some of the members of our family, The Hallelujah Trail Players, who attended our picnic. You may have seen them around the baked bean casserole. Now we see them struggling along the Hallelujah Trail with some leftovers. As ants usually do, they make their whereabouts known by singing to each other.

(ANTRON *enters stage left, slowly struggles his way to center stage. He tugs at a piece of heavy celery while turning to look back.*)

ANTRON: Humm. Come on, Anteleven, you can make it.

(ANTELEVEN *shuffles on, stage left, carrying leaves and a huge baked bean. He heaves his way to the medium cube and sits down, breathing a sigh of relief.*)

ANTELEVEN: Humm. Made it! Whew! That was quite a picnic.

ANTRON: Humm. The beans were superb. *(Sits on large cube)*

ANTELEVEN: *(Tries to pat his stomach)* Humm. And the stuffed celery stuffed me.

ANTRON: Humm. We made a haul for the Leafeater family reunion.

ANTRIX: *(Still seated front row to the left of the stage)* Bloo dah.

ANTRON: Humm. Anteleven, listen. . . . What was that?

(ANTRIX *rises and moves to the stage.*)

ANTELEVEN: Humm. Sounds like someone said gloo du.

ANTRIX: Bloo dah.

ANTELEVEN: Humm. Not one of our sounds. Be careful.

ANTRON: Humm. I think I've seen her before. I think her name is Antrix!

ANTELEVEN: Humm. Take a load off.

(ANTRIX *sits on the smallest of the cubes.*)

ANTRON: Humm. Where you headed?

ANTRIX: Bloo dah. Glory Hill Storage. How about you?

ANTRON: Humm. We're collecting food for the Leafeater family reunion.

ANTELEVEN: It's next Saturday. Humm.

ANTRIX: Bloo dah. How many mouths to feed?

ANTRON: Humm. Ninety-two.

ANTRIX:	Bloo dah. You're kidding! I'm a Harvester ant. Do you know how many would come to the Harvester family reunion?
ANTRON:	Humm. How many?
ANTRIX:	Bloo dah. Exactly four. The Harvester ants were almost killed off by the new Slug-A-Bug Insecticide.
ANTELEVEN:	Humm. Sorry. Who's left in your family?
ANTRIX:	Bloo dah. Only Father, Grandmother, Uncle Pickett, and myself.
ANTRON:	Humm. Look at it this way. Every time you eat a meal together, it's a family reunion. *(Laughs)* What a deal!
ANTELEVEN:	Humm. I'll bet they skip the "my how you've grown" bit. Besides, you don't have to remember thirty-zillion names.
ANTRIX:	Bloo dah. Thanks for trying to cheer me up, but I'd love to belong to a huggin', kissin', backslappin', and laughin' family.
ANTELEVEN:	Humm. If your family is so little, why do you go around bloo dahing all the time? No one's out following you on the trail.
	(ANTRIX steps back, stands motionless thinking it over, then yells.)
ANTRIX:	BLOO DAH!
ANTELEVEN:	Humm. Didn't mean to insult you. I'm sorry!
ANTRIX:	Bloo dah.
	(Offstage the uncle ants softly warm up their humms.)
ANTRIX:	*(Loudly, over the warm up humms)* Bloo dahing is a Harvester ritual. We have to watch out for each other, so we keep in touch.
	(UNCLE SCOTT and UNCLE JEFF shuffle onstage left, moving to center next to ANTRON.)
UNCLE SCOTT:	Humm. Greetings, Anteleven. Antron.
ANTRON and ANTELEVEN:	Humm. Greetings.
UNCLE JEFF:	*(Points to leaf on the floor)* Is that yours?
ANTRON:	Humm. No.
	(UNCLE JEFF picks up the leaf and exits stage right with UNCLE SCOTT shuffling along behind, while UNCLE JEREMIAH, UNCLE LEWIS, UNCLE ROBERT, and UNCLE PAUL shuffle in, stage left. They are humming.)

ANTELEVEN:	Humm. Hi, uncles.
UNCLE JEREMIAH, **UNCLE LEWIS,** **UNCLE ROBERT,** **and UNCLE PAUL:**	Humm. Humm.

(They look ANTRIX over cautiously, then gather behind ANTRON. UNCLE PAUL speaks while the other uncles feel ANTRIX's antennae.)

UNCLE PAUL: Humm. Who's that?

ANTRON: Humm. Meet Antrix Harvester from Glory Hill.

(The uncles gasp at the name Glory Hill. They begin to pat ANTRIX comfortingly.)

UNCLE LEWIS: Sorry about the Slug-A-Bug.

UNCLE ROBERT: Humm. Are you all alone?

ANTRIX: There are four of us.

(The uncles groan. One wipes a tear. They put their heads together in a circle (with difficulty) and humm on and on. Finally, they break away. UNCLE ROBERT steps in front of ANTRIX.)

UNCLE ROBERT: Humm. Ahem. *(Clears throat again)* We invite you to the Leafeater family reunion. Come, if you puhhhhhleese.

ANTRIX: Bloo dah. But I'm not family.

(The uncles confer again, heads together with much humming.)

UNCLE ROBERT: Humm. You're not a Leafeater, but you're in our . . . our . . . circle.

(All the Leafeaters nod heads again and again.)

ANTRIX: *(Softly)* Bloo dah. Your circle?

UNCLE ROBERT: You're God's family. You know, all creatures created by him, loved by him, and all that stuff.

ANTRIX: Bloo dah. I'll ask Father about coming. But he may feel we're outsiders.

ANTELEVEN: Humm. *(Laughing)* Just tell him we're all one family in the ant hill of life.

(Everyone either groans or laughs.)

UNCLE LEWIS: *(Looking expectantly into ANTRIX'S face)* And . . . Humm. Will you teach us how to make that gloo du sound?

ANTRIX: *(Nodding yes)* Bloo dah. Yes.

(The uncles nod individually to ANTRIX, ANTRON, and ANTELEVEN, then shuffle march exit stage right humming softly as UNCLE AL and UNCLE BILL enter, humming, stage left. They pass across upstage, pausing only to speak.)

UNCLE AL:	Humm. Hello, Antron *(Nods to ANTRON)*, Anteleven *(Nods to ANTELEVEN)*.
ANTELEVEN:	Humm. Hi, Uncle Al and . . . and . . . Uncle . . . *(Looks to ANTRON for help with the name.)*
	(ANTRON shrugs his shoulders. UNCLE AL and UNCLE BILL shuffle exit stage right.)
ANTRIX:	*(Moving closer to ANTRON)* You don't know your own uncle's name?
ANTRON:	Humm. *(Confidentially)* Since my parents divorced and married again, I don't know everyone.
ANTRIX:	Why not?
ANTELEVEN:	He has sisters and step-sisters and . . .
ANTRON:	The six brothers and five sisters I can name. It's the twelve uncles and eight grandmothers that puzzle me. Three grandmas live in California and two in Oregon.
ANTELEVEN:	The only time we see *everybody* is at the family reunion. In between, sometimes we argue, sometimes we visit, and sometimes we just ignore each other.
ANTRIX:	Bloo dah. How do you keep them straight?
ANTRON:	Humm. I don't. If they humm, I hug them.
	(All the grandmother and uncle ants in the audience begin humming. ANTRON looks up in surprise.)
ANTRON:	Humm. Hear that? *(They listen. Humming stops)* They're out there all right. What a huge, crazy, mixed up family.
ANTELEVEN:	Careful. I'm your first cousin. Remember every family is different from the next one.
ANTRON:	I hope other families don't have twelve uncles to remember—especially at Christmas.
	(Ants from audience begin humming, then start applause as ANTRON, ANTRIX, and ANTELEVEN shuffle exit stage right struggling under their heavy loads.)

OPTIONAL SHARING TIME

If the group is large, divide into smaller groups, keeping family Love-Units together. Because you know the needs of your congregation, you will be able to slant the discussion by the questions you choose—questions concerning families, conflict in families, or the church as a family. If you have young children in the group, select easy, concrete questions. The playlet adapts well to extended discussion of family understanding and issues, but it also can highlight the family community of your church.

DISCUSSION QUESTIONS

Families:

1. How many grandmothers do you have? Are some of them great-great grandmothers? Are there any grandmothers in the group? How many grandchildren do they have?
2. What do you like to do when you are with your grandmothers? Grandmothers who are deceased are also a great part of our lives, so you might say what did you like to do with them?
3. Family units are all different. Who lives in your home at the present time?
4. What do you do for each other? Antron and Anteleven were members of a blended family, that is one in which one nuclear parent, his or her children, his or her spouse, and that spouse's children live together. Do the things you do for each other change when you move from a nuclear to blended family? Read Colossians 3:12-17 for further ideas about working and relating in the family.

Conflict in Families:

5. All families have occasional disagreements. Family arguments often center around: (1) money, (2) relatives (in-laws and step-families), and (3) use of time. Please share your ideas about successful settlement of conflicts in these areas.
6. Some conflicts get out of hand. What church family resources might be of help to a family in which there is violence or emotional discord? (If evidence of violence surfaces during the discussion, make a point of dealing with it privately. Abuse and violence cannot be ignored. Love dares to help find a solution to abuse and other forms of violence.)

The Church as a Family:

7. How many people are in your church family? Think of the church family as being beyond the Love-Units of this event. The church is a place where everyone belongs, and where people love and support each other. This is church family—a circle of love drawing everyone in.
8. How was Antrix different from the Leafeaters? Are there differences in our church family? There may be racial, theological, intellectual, social, economic, and physical differences. A church family knows about differences, and plans for individual needs, but a circle of love considers all persons children of God.
9. Anteleven was cautious about the stranger, Antrix. How do we hold back from strangers in our church family? How do we reach out to strangers?
10. Ants really sing to maintain contact with each other. The Leafeater Ants hummed and the Harvester Ant bloo dahed. How do we, in our church family, stay in touch with each other?
11. Ant families sing to each other. Discuss and try out your own family Love-Unit singing sound. This sound will be made in the closing circle.
12. What do people in your church family do for each other?

For an Older Group:

Read and discuss the following scriptures, keeping the words *family* and *church family* in mind: Col. 3:12-25, Phil. 4:8, I Cor. 13:4-7 and 13, Deut. 5:6-21 or Exod. 20:1-7, and Matt. 22:37-40.

CELEBRATE CHURCH FAMILY

Make a ring of love with all participants of this intergenerational event. Do it even if it has to go down the hall, around the corner, and back. There's something about holding hands in a ring that shows inclusiveness and the power of love.

LEADER: We celebrate every person who has come here to be part of the church family. Stomp your feet if you want to celebrate. *(Stomping time)*

LEADER: We celebrate our family Love-Units and give thanks for getting closer to other persons in that family. Clap your hands if you want to celebrate. *(Clapping time)*

LEADER: We celebrate the warm feeling of being in the circle of God's love. Hold hands in the circle and squeeze hands if you want to celebrate. *(Hand squeezing in silence)*

LEADER: As we say goodbye, we celebrate our differences and unity as we make our love-family sounds. Make your sound if you want to celebrate. *(Sound-making time)*

LEADER: Goodbye.

EVENT THEME: IT'S LOVE

BASED ON I CORINTHIANS 13, MICAH 6:8, AND ROMANS 13:8-10.

SCHEDULE

*Get nametags.
*Get Together Activities:
    1. Write a wall of Christian love.
    2. Dinner and singing of "For the Beauty of the Earth" (p. 29), and other songs about love.
    3. Award a prize for the person who has hugged the most.
*Focus Activity:
    1. Presentation of video drama "The Epidemic."
*Sharing Time:
    1. Group discussion (optional).
    2. If the group is older, have closing worship.
    3. If the group is younger, play the game "Pass It On."

ADVANCE PREPARATION

*Recruit a moderator.
*Recruit a song leader and make copies of music.
*Recruit a video drama chairperson.
*For a small group, obtain a VCR and television. For a large group, obtain a large screen television, or divide into smaller groups, each with a television set and VCR. If you elect the latter method, copy enough video tapes for each group's television.
    Alternate plan: Film the drama in still shots with a 35 millimeter camera, tape record script and sound, and use a slide projector and large screen.
*Cover a wall with paper and write the following instructions at the top: Write ways to say you love someone or ways you show your love. As a way of encouraging others, write something on the paper yourself.
*If the group is large, and you plan discussion after the drama, recruit discussion leaders.

*If the group is young, select a game leader.
*Select a secret, qualified observer to buy a hugability prize beforehand and present it to the person who hugs the most persons before dinner.

ROOM ARRANGEMENT

*Place the nametag table near the graffiti wall. Put marking pens on the table. Test the paper. Does ink bleed through? If so, consider crayons.
*Set up the televisions you have elected to use.

AS PEOPLE ARRIVE

*Get nametags and write or draw pictures on the graffiti sheet.

FOCUS ACTIVITY

THE EPIDEMIC
A video drama about a love epidemic.

Production Notes

Characters: Dr. Boss, male or female about forty; Mr. Humbug, male, any age; a school room filled with twenty or thirty fourth-grade children; their teacher, Ms. Hamilton, any age; five senior citizens, Ben, Ralph, Alice, Bea, Andy; Dr. David, about thirty-five; Mr. Smith and his two children; a dog; Reverend Kidd, male or female, any age. (Yes, the cast is large, but each brief scene is filled separately. The dog and children do not have speaking parts. Recruiting staff and actors and finding shoot locations is a very big part of the publicity for this event.)

Playing Time: Approximately 10–15 minutes.

Properties: "The Rash" material for Scenes II, IV, and VI. Use gummed valentine hearts or cut small hearts from red construction paper and stick them on with double-sided transparent tape. *Do not use marking pens,* unless you want a permanent rash.

Scene I: A door labeled "Plague County Health Director," two desks, two desk chairs, two telephones, stacks of paper, two desk placards, "Dr. Boss" and "Mr. Humbug."

Scene II: A school classroom with small desks, a teacher's desk, and books for desks. Shoot this on location at a school or in the church school.

Scene III: Repeat of Scene I.

Scene IV: A card table and five or six chairs. Dominoes.

Scene V: Repeat of Scene I.

Scene VI: Shoot at a veterinary clinic or use a high table at the church.

Scene VII: Repeat of Scene I.

Costumes:

Scene I: Dr. Boss, white doctor's coat; the secretary, appropriate office clothing.

Scene II: School clothing.

Scene III: Repeat Scene I.

Scene IV: Casual clothing.

Scene V: Repeat Scene I.

Scene VI: Mr. Smith and children are dressed casually. Dr. Davis wears a white lab coat.

Scene VII: Repeat Scene I except minister wears costume of your local church.

Equipment Needed: A camcorder with a built-in microphone, zoom lens, and electronic viewfinder. If your camcorder does not have a character generator, make posters and shoot them close up. If your camcorder does not have editing capability, use two camcorders and two video tapes for editing; this method takes more time than you think, so start early. A TV set on which to show the finished film. If using several sets, make copies of your video. A video cassette record (VCR) for each television set.

Staff needed:

1. A video drama director.
2. A camcorder operator, preferably experienced.
3. A set manager or managers to arrange for locations and get them ready for shooting.
4. A properties manager.

Copy script for all staff and actors. Meet with the cast for a read-through. Then rehearse the lines and practice body language. Film a rehearsal so the cast can see how it works and how they look on camera. Memorized lines are a must, but fear not—all segments are short.

THE EPIDEMIC

Shot One: Title—"The Epidemic"
Use character generator on camcorder, or hold the camera on the prepared printed title about twice as long as it takes to read it.
Shot Two: Credits
List the names of the director, camera operator, actors, and location set directors.

Scene I

Shot Three: Fade In.
Long shot to establish setting—Use the city limit sign of your town.
Shot Four: Interior Hallway.
Zoom to an office door bearing the sign "Plague County Health Department." The door opens revealing an office with a desk belonging to Dr. Boss.
Shot Five: Interior Office.
We see a neat desk containing only a telephone, a stack of papers, a pencil caddy with pencils, and a nameplate with the name Dr. Boss.
Shot Six: Short Shot on Dr. Boss.
The doctor is methodical, clinical, and is neatly dressed in the white coat of a

doctor. He seems puzzled and turns a paper over and over looking for something he has missed. The telephone rings; he answers it absentmindedly.

DR. BOSS: Dr. Boss here. *(Pause)* We're doing everything we can, Commissioner. *(Pause)* I know the press is after you. They bother me, too, but we don't have a single lead. *(Pause)* Yes, I'll let you know. *(Pause)* Yes. Yes. Goodbye.

(He hangs up the phone, and has not removed his hand until it rings again. He pulls his hand away quickly as if the phone is hot. When the phone finally stops ringing, he punches a button on the phone and speaks.)

DR. BOSS: Hold my calls, Mr. Humbug. I need time to think.

(The off-camera voice of MR. HUMBUG *answers.)*

MR. HUMBUG: Things are stacking up, *Sir.* There are troubles everywhere. You'd better see to it, *Sir.*

DR. BOSS: I'll come out. But hold the calls.

MR. HUMBUG: Yes, sir.

Shot Seven: Mr. Humbug's office.
Medium Shot on MR. HUMBUG *sitting at his desk behind two stacks of reports, each about one foot in height.* MR. HUMBUG *is the perfect, polished secretary, but a little bossy and very sarcastic. He would like to run things with an iron hand, and it is obvious there is friction between himself and his boss.*

MR. HUMBUG: The paper work is getting ahead of you, *Sir.*

Shot Eight: Wider angle of Mr. Humbug's office.
The angle now includes DR. BOSS, MR. HUMBUG, *and part of their surroundings.*

DR. BOSS: I'm well aware of that. What kind of trouble do we have?

MR. HUMBUG: Complaints from all over _____ *(your town).*

DR. BOSS: About?

MR. HUMBUG: About the rash.

DR. BOSS: You mean more about *the* rash of rashes?

MR. HUMBUG: Yes! Look at the stack. *(MR. HUMBUG selects a paper and holds it up to* DR. BOSS *for inspection.)* This one is from the Lady Be Lovely cosmetic store. They haven't made a sale in three days. All their customers have rashes, and they are so busy helping each other they don't have time to spend money. They're afraid to put makeup on rashy skin.

DR. BOSS: Who's next?

MR. HUMBUG: *(MR. HUMBUG picks up another piece of paper.)* This one's from the school. There's a rash there, too.

DR. BOSS: Lots of absences?

MR. HUMBUG: Absences? Look for yourself. *(MR. HUMBUG hands* DR. BOSS *the report.)*

Scene II

Shot Nine: Interior of school room.
Twenty or thirty fourth-grade school children are milling around their desks in an elementary school room. Their teacher, MS. HAMILTON, stands in front of the room, near her desk. Each student is covered with a red rash.

MS. HAMILTON: Take your seats and be quiet, please.

                     (The children move toward their seats, although some take time to hug MS. HAMILTON, and at various times they tell her they love her. She acts surprised.)

Shot Ten: Shot from teacher's desk.
Over the shoulder shot showing smiling children seated neatly at attention with books open.

Shot Eleven: Close up Ms. Hamilton's face.
MS. HAMILTON'*s face shows that the children's behavior is incredulous. She now wears the heart rash. She breaks into a broad smile.*

Scene III

Shot Twelve: Mr. Humbug's office.
MR. HUMBUG *snatches the report from* DR. BOSS's *hand.*

MR. HUMBUG: Wasn't that disgusting!

DR. BOSS: Looked peaceful to me. Except that the teacher caught the rash. What is the complaint?

MR. HUMBUG: With no discipline problems and the children working so hard, all the teachers ran out of lesson plans. The bus drivers had to take the children home early. The bus drivers were so happy that *they* broke out in The Rash.

DR. BOSS: Very contagious. Any details?

MR. HUMBUG: No, only more reports.

DR. BOSS: Who's next.

MR. HUMBUG: (MR. HUMBUG *picks up another report, and reads it for a minute.)* The trade union boss called. All the negotiators turned up with The Rash. They voted down a strike call. She reported they voted to have a company picnic to . . . let's see how they said it . . . oh, yes *(Reading)* to play ball and learn to be team players.

DR. BOSS: Did the union boss catch The Rash?

MR. HUMBUG: Not yet. She doesn't know if it's contagious.

DR. BOSS: Put her in quarantine so we can observe the incubation period.

MR. HUMBUG:	You sure, *Sir?*
DR. BOSS:	I said quarantine!
MR. HUMBUG:	*(Dials a telephone number, and waits)* Mrs. Union Boss, please. *(Pauses)* No, thank you. No message. *(MR. HUMBUG hangs up the phone and sits silently a minute.)*
DR. BOSS:	Well?
MR. HUMBUG:	She's not there, Sir. She's gone to the picnic.
DR. BOSS:	Make a note of that on the report. What other complaints have been filed?
MR. HUMBUG:	Here's one from the Autumn Hills Retirement Center. *(MR. HUMBUG hands the report to DR. BOSS, who stands reading it.)*
DR. BOSS:	The Rash is there! This rash is of epidemic proportions.

Scene IV

Shot Thirteen: Retirement Center recreation room.
(Senior citizens RALPH (has The Rash), BEN, ALICE (has The Rash), and BEA (has The Rash) are seated playing dominoes. ANDY stands nearby looking on. He edges closer.)

RALPH:	You cut off my play!
BEN:	So I did.
RALPH:	Oh, well, you made a fair play.
BEN:	What?
RALPH:	Fair play.
BEN:	Aren't you going to argue with me?
	(ANDY edges closer to stand between BEN and BEA.)
RALPH:	No.
BEN:	Heck. It's no fun without a fight!
ALICE:	More fun for us. We get tired of listening to you bicker and argue all the time, don't we, Bea?
	(BEA makes a place for ANDY.)
BEA:	Yes. Ben, you say the ugliest things. You make me feel little.
BEN:	I didn't know.
BEA:	You do now. *(Turns to ANDY)* Pull up a chair and play dominoes with us.

Shot Fourteen: Close up of Ben and Bea.
Ben leans near Bea's ear and speaks confidentially.

BEN: Hush, Bea. We've been a foursome for two years.

BEA: I know. But five can play dominoes.

BEN: But we're a club.

BEA: *(Loudly)* We're friends who play together. There's always room for a new friend.

                (ANDY *drags up a chair and places it between* BEN *and* BEA. *He draws some dominoes.*)

ANDY: Thanks. I'd like to play.

Scene V

Shot Fifteen: Broad shot of Mr. Humbug and Dr. Boss at Mr. Humbug's desk.

MR. HUMBUG: *(Snorts)* A bunch of foolishness if you ask me! That rash makes people do silly things.

DR. BOSS: What was the complaint out there?

MR. HUMBUG: The social director filed the complaint. With all the friendliness going around, the residents found ways to entertain themselves. The social director is looking for another job.

DR. BOSS: Any other Rash reports?

MR. HUMBUG: There was one from Family Service Center, who reported child abuse was down.

DR. BOSS: That's good news.

MR. HUMBUG: The bad news is they've had more calls then they can handle for counseling troubled parents. The director mumbled something about love wanting to find a way to avoid violence. Makes no sense.

DR. BOSS: Humm.

MR. HUMBUG: Here's a report from a veterinarian named Dr. Davis. Read it for yourself.

                (DR. BOSS *takes the paper, reads it, and stands shaking his head in disbelief.*)

Scene VI

Shot Sixteen: Interior of veterinary clinic.
Angle on DR. DAVIS *who stands next to an examination table. On the table is a small dog that has The Rash.*

DR. DAVIS:	There, now your dog's paw will feel better. It's strange that he has a rash. This is the seventh case I've seen today. Even the Taylor's cat, who was hit by a car, had it. The Taylors had it, too.

Shot Seventeen: Wide angle to examining table.
Standing next to the table are MR. SMITH *and* TWO CHILDREN.

MR. SMITH:	Have you looked in a mirror lately?
DR. DAVIS:	No. Do I have it, too?
MR. SMITH:	Yes.
DR. DAVIS:	*(Feeling his face)* It doesn't hurt. And I feel great. Funny thing, though, now that everyone has The Rash, my business has fallen off.

Scene VII

Shot Eighteen: Close angle of Dr. Boss and Mr. Humbug.
DR. BOSS *still stands next to* MR. HUMBUG's *desk looking through papers.*

DR. BOSS:	Not one rash victim complains of illness.
MR. HUMBUG:	*(Leafing through papers)* No.
DR. BOSS:	Have you checked the hospitals?
MR. HUMBUG:	*(Indignantly)* Of course, *Sir.*
	(DR. BOSS *pulls a chair in close to* MR. HUMBUG's *desk, pulls some papers close to him and begins to leaf through them.)*
MR. HUMBUG:	*(Retrieves the papers)* If you please, *Sir.*
DR. BOSS:	I was merely trying to find out the dates.
MR. HUMBUG:	What dates, *Sir?*
DR. BOSS:	Don't get in a snit, Mr. Humbug. I want to know when this all started.
MR. HUMBUG:	Obvious, *Sir,* last weekend.
	(A knock is heard and REVEREND KIDD enters the office.)
REVEREND KIDD:	Hey, Dr. Boss. You ready to go to lunch?
	(DR. BOSS looks up in surprise and gasps.)
DR. BOSS:	Oh, no! You caught The Rash.
REVEREND KIDD:	What?
DR. BOSS:	Reverend Kidd, you caught The Rash, too.
REVEREND KIDD:	Broke out last Sunday. About 11:45 I started to feel warm.

DR. BOSS:	Right in church? No wonder everyone has it. You exposed the whole church.
MR. HUMBUG:	*(Sarcastically)* Those of you who went to church.
REVEREND KIDD:	No. Most of my congregation had it as they left.

Shot Nineteen: Close up of Reverend Kidd showing The Rash.

DR. BOSS:	What happened during church? Any mold or fungus in the air conditioning that could cause an allergic reaction?
REVEREND KIDD:	The whole thing happened because of my sermon.

Shot Twenty: Wide angle showing Reverend Kidd, Dr. Boss, and Mr. Humbug.

MR. HUMBUG:	*(Muttering)* Now I've heard everything.
DR. BOSS:	You're kidding.
REVEREND KIDD:	Would I kid you? All I said was that we should start a love epidemic. I told everyone to look in the mirror every morning and say, "I love God. God loves me. I love others. I love myself." It just took off from there. They didn't wait for mirrors, just thinking those thoughts made them break out. It's almost an epidemic.
DR. BOSS:	*(Loudly)* And I just spent five days trying to find the cause and cure of your epidemic.
REVEREND KIDD:	It's not my epidemic. It's God's. And don't you dare cure it! I spent a year preaching, trying to get people thinking this way.
MR. HUMBUG:	Bah, humbug. I don't believe it.

Shot Twenty-one: Shot of paper in Dr. Boss's hand.
Shot over DR. BOSS's *shoulder as he turns over the paper, which is covered with hearts.*

DR. BOSS:	I believe it.

DISCUSSION QUESTIONS

Select questions appropriate for your group. If the group contains small children, remember their short attention span and need to move their bodies.
  1. According to the playlet, what does love do? (Changes lives, makes us forgive others, makes us inclusive, makes us look for peaceful solutions to conflicts, and adds depth to life's experiences. There will be other answers. People will answer according to their needs.)
  2. What changed the community? If it was a team effort, who was on the team?
  3. Is a love epidemic realistic? How has anyone in the group tried loving others with successful results?

4. What should a Christian do if love doesn't improve the relationship or situation?
5. How do you think Mr. Humbug felt inside? Is there a cure for Humbug?
6. Pass out Bibles and have everyone silently read I Corinthians 13:4-7. If yours is a group without reading skills, ask for a volunteer to read. After reading, pantomime (act out without words) ways you, or someone you know, might love. Use contrasts like those suggested in I Corinthians, such as rude versus polite, patient rather than cross, or jealous as opposed to loving and sharing. Show each other solutions to life's everyday problems.
7. An older, or more theologically astute, group might consider I John 3:14, "He who does not love remains in death." Discuss what kind of death that might indicate.

CLOSING WORSHIP

Either seated or in a standing circle, divide the group into four sections. Each group will begin whispering the word *love* when you tell it to. Experiment with the softness of the whispering, and have each group try saying the word while listening to you. Play with the group, and practice whispers of love. When you are ready to begin, point to the first group, listen to their whispers a few seconds; point to the second group to join them, listen a few seconds; point to the third group to join the first two groups, listen a few seconds; and then add the fourth group. When the whisper of love has spread across everyone, let them continue while you read loudly the following:

> *I love God*
> *God loves me.*
> *I love others.*
> *I love myself.*

Now reverse the whispers one section at a time until only one breath of whispering remains. Say, "Amen."

OPTIONAL CLOSING GAME

Pass It On

Seat players in a circle.

The object of the game is to pass an action and/or a phrase completely around the circle without anyone breaking the chain by forgetting an action. The person who breaks the chain is out of the circle.

A designated player begins by saying, "I love you—pass it on." The second person says I love you and adds something such as "stomp your feet—pass it on." The third person says, "I love you—stomp your feet, and wave your hand—pass it on." The fourth person says, "I love you—stomp your feet, wave your hand, and nod your head—pass it on." Everyone in the circle says something to add and repeats everything said until someone breaks the chain. Play moves past that person, who is removed from the circle.

For the Beauty of the Earth

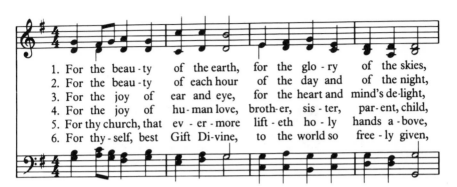

1. For the beau-ty   of the earth,   for the glo-ry   of the skies,
2. For the beau-ty   of each hour   of the day and   of the night,
3. For the joy   of   ear and eye,   for the heart and mind's de-light,
4. For the joy   of   hu-man love,   broth-er, sis-ter,   par-ent, child,
5. For thy church, that ev - er - more   lift - eth ho - ly   hands a - bove,
6. For thy-self, best   Gift Di-vine,   to the world so   free - ly given,

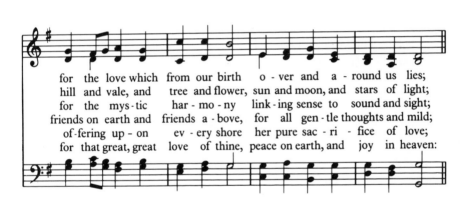

for   the love which from our birth   o - ver and a - round us lies;
hill and vale, and   tree and flower, sun and moon, and stars of light;
for   the mys-tic   har - mo - ny   link-ing sense to sound and sight;
friends on earth and friends a - bove, for all gen-tle thoughts and mild;
of-fering up - on   ev - ery shore her pure sac - ri - fice of love;
for that great, great   love of thine, peace on earth, and   joy in heaven:

Refrain

    Lord of all, to   thee   we raise this our hymn of   grate-ful praise.
* *Christ, our God, to   thee   we raise   this our sac - ri - fice of praise.*

WORDS: Folliot S. Pierpoint, 1864
MUSIC: Conrad Kocher, 1838; arr. by W. H. Monk, 1861

EVENT THEME:
RESOLVING CONFLICT

SCHEDULE

*Get nametags.
*Focus Activity:
   1. Playlet, "The Oleo Lovely Laundromat" or
   2. Skit, "Perspective."
*Have dinner or refreshments.
*Sharing time:
   1. Preface by Moderator.
   2. Role-playing and/or discussion in groups.
*Closing.

This event works well as part of a retreat or series when used with the "Peace" event, p. 41.

ADVANCE PREPARATION

Conflict is a normal part of everyday life. Some apparent conflicts, however, cause disruption and tension in personal and community lives. Let representatives from each age group help you focus this event according to your knowledge of these apparent conflicts, or focus this event to bring certain conflicts to light for discussion.

Consider linking the setting of the event you are planning with other resources in your community, especially local schools. The videocassette series *Magic Circle Conflict Curriculum* includes "Kids in Conflict" (for teachers), "The Pinch" (for elementary grade children about conflicts and anger), and "Bleacher Feature" (for upper elementary grade children about doing right and getting in trouble anyway). "Young Peacemakers," a twenty minute videocassette is usable for any age group, but is set with older children and youth. It includes the use of some of the mediation techniques suggested in "The Oleo Lovely Laundromat." These videocassettes are available from Ecufilm, 810 12th Avenue South, Nashville, Tennessee 37203.

*Recruit a moderator.
*Recruit a director for drama.
*Select and train small group leaders.
*Plan menu and arrange preparation.
*Order videocassettes, if you plan to use them.

ROOM ARRANGEMENT

*A table for nametags.
*Arrange chairs in front of staging area. If possible, set the staging area near a door that can be incorporated for exits and entrances.

AS PEOPLE ARRIVE

*Get nametags.
*The moderator directs persons to staging area. The interesting stage setting focuses attention.

FOCUS ACTIVITY

THE OLEO LOVELY LAUNDROMAT
Playlet

Production Notes

Characters: Moderator, Mrs. Oleo Lovely (over twenty-five), Julie (mother of Pat and Elaine), Pat (boy eight to twelve), Elaine (child any age), Al (forty to ninety).

Playing time: About 8 minutes.

Properties: Sorting table, TV tray used as a magazine table, clothes rack, two laundry baskets filled with laundry, a bright red shirt, laundry soap granules, measuring cups, shipping boxes made into washers and dryers (use magic markers and cut holes in front so that clothes may be removed), chairs, magazines, a large sign that reads "The Oleo Lovely Laundromat" over the folding table, and two smaller signs in appropriate places that read "Washers 75 cents" and "Dryers 50 cents."

Costumes: Casual attire. Mrs. Oleo Lovely wears an apron.

Setting: The Oleo Lovely Laundromat, owned by Oleo Lovely. Against a wall at stage right is a bank of washers and dryers. Two rows of chairs, back-to-back, are arranged from upstage to downstage. A small table at the downstage end of the row of chairs has magazines lying on it. There also are magazines on some of the chairs. A cup of soap granules is on a chair near Al. A long sorting table and hanging rack are stage left.

(Performers are frozen in place as MODERATOR makes introduction, then turn to action. AL is seated center stage reading a magazine. PAT and ELAINE move on opposite sides of the row of chairs. JULIE stands by a washer staring off into space, ignoring the noise they are making.)

MODERATOR: The theme of our event is resolving conflict. There are many ways to resolve conflict. With the help of The Squeaky Clean Players, we will examine one of these ways.

PAT: *(Running around chairs)* Can't catch me!

ELAINE: *(Chasing PAT)* Can to. Watch me.

PAT: Catch this!

(PAT snatches a magazine from a chair and throws it to ELAINE who misses. The magazine hits AL who shifts in his chair, clears his throat, and then goes on reading.)

ELAINE: Uh oh. *(Singsong)* You're in trouble. Gonna tell.

(PAT falls into a chair and is instantly still while ELAINE runs toward him as JULIE suddenly notices a problem.)

JULIE: Elaine! Stop tearing up the place.

ELAINE: I didn't do anything.

PAT: Did too.

ELAINE: Don't blame me. Pat did it.

JULIE: You *(Pointing at ELAINE)* sit down and behave yourself. We're almost finished. This last shirt is ready for the dryer.

(ELAINE sits next to PAT. JULIE removes a bright red shirt from box washer and places it in a box dryer.)

JULIE: Pat, please don't buy any more fading shirts. Washing one thing at a time is expensive. *(Searching pocket for money)* Elaine, do you have two quarters?

ELAINE: I'm broke.

JULIE: Pat?

PAT: Huh?

JULIE: I need two quarters to dry your shirt.

PAT: I spent mine at the soft drink machine. Ask Mrs. Lovely.

JULIE: *(Walking toward the folding table)* She's not here. You two behave yourselves while I go next door for change. *(Exits stage left)*

PAT: *(Jumps up running)* Last one to the window is a chicken.

(ELAINE races toward downstage center. She knocks a full cup of soap granules to the floor, where it scatters.)

AL: *(Jumping up)* Now look what you've done.

(MRS. LOVELY enters stage left carrying a load of clothes, which she dumps on the table. She begins folding them as ELAINE and PAT quietly sit in chairs.)

AL: You! Get over here and pick this up.

(ELAINE and PAT sit motionless.)

AL: Come on, you brats, you spilled it!

AL: *(ELAINE and PAT try to pick it up, but end up scattering it more than ever. AL takes his clothes from a dryer, puts them in a basket, and takes them to the dryer containing JULIE's red shirt. He takes the shirt out, and pitches it toward a chair, but it falls on the floor in the soap. He puts his laundry in the dryer, places coins in the slot, and sits down.)*

AL: Put the soap back where you got it. And sit down and shut up. Every week you're in here tearing up the magazines and spilling soda and soap.

(ELAINE and PAT do not sit down. JULIE enters stage left.)

AL: I said sit down and shut up. *(Yelling)* You're acting like hooligans! *(Sit down)*

JULIE: No need to yell.

AL: They're tearing up the place.

JULIE: And they're not hooligans! *(Goes to dryer with her coins, discovers AL's clothes there, turns to face AL)* Where's my red shirt?

AL: *(Points)* On the chair.

JULIE: On the floor! *(Yells)* Thanks for nothing.

AL: How did I know it was yours?

JULIE: Anyone else here? *(Stands in front of AL looking down at him)*

AL: Just two rowdy kids.

JULIE: *(Yells)* Rowdy?

AL: Why don't you teach your kids some manners? *(AL stands up, causing JULIE to step back to avoid being knocked over.)*

JULIE: Manners? Is it good manners to steal a dryer and throw my shirt on the floor?

AL: Better manners than tying up the last dryer while you run all over creation looking for change. *(Louder)* You do that every week. I watch you do it *every single week!*

PAT: She does not.

ELAINE:	We bring money every week.
JULIE:	They're right.
AL:	Keep your brats out of this!
JULIE:	Don't blame them. *(Slaps* AL *across the cheek)* And don't ever call my children brats!

(MRS. LOVELY runs to stand between AL and JULIE.)

MRS. LOVELY:	Wait! This is out of hand.

(Everyone stands silent and motionless.)

MRS. LOVELY:	Unless you sit down quietly, someone may call the police. *(Arranges five chairs around the magazine table with the open side to the audience.)* Well, sit down.

(They all sit down, but glare at each other.)

MRS. LOVELY:	You know me as Mrs. Lovely, the owner. My first name is Oleo. Please call me Oleo.

(PAT and ELAINE snicker.)

MRS. LOVELY:	This is going to be a serious circle. We need to be on a first name basis. *(to* AL) What's yours?
MRS. LOVELY:	Al.
JULIE:	Julie.
PAT:	*(Shrugs)*
MRS. LOVELY:	*(gently)* Come on, now.
PAT:	Pat.
ELAINE:	Elaine.
MRS. LOVELY:	If I hadn't intervened, we could have had real violence here. Lots of trouble.
AL:	Slapping is violent.
JULIE:	I'm sorry, really sorry. Things just got out of hand. But you didn't . . . *(Clenches her fists then drops them to her lap)*
MRS. LOVELY:	We're looking for a solution, not blame.
PAT:	But he called us brats.
ELAINE:	And hooligans, whatever that is.
MRS. LOVELY:	First off, in this circle there will be no name calling. Agreed?

(Everyone nods affirmatively.)

MRS. LOVELY:	Next, a solution instead of blame means that instead of saying "he has a problem" or "she has a problem," we are going to say, "*we* have a problem. *Our* problem caused

conflict." At the same time, each one accepts responsibility for his or her actions.

(JULIE, AL, PAT, *and* ELAINE *stare at her in amazement. They look at each other and shrug.*)

MRS. LOVELY: Conflict and violence can get out of hand. *(*MRS. LOVELY *looks directly at* JULIE *who looks at the clenched fists in her own lap.)*

MRS. LOVELY: But I want to help you have a feeling that you can do something about this. You aren't helpless.

JULIE: How? How can *you* help?

MRS. LOVELY: First, each person—without being interrupted—will say his or her idea of the conflict. Then we will speak directly back and forth. Then we will agree to try a different way of relating next week when you do your laundry. Who will be first?

(Silence)

MRS. LOVELY: Usually, the mediator doesn't become involved in stating the problem, but since you're new at this and my place of business is involved, I'll speak. Our problem from my point of view is that every Thursday morning, Al, Julie, and the children arrive at the same time to do their laundry. They must share equipment. *(Pause)* Who will be next?

ELAINE: There's nothing to do here. We've read all the magazines.

PAT: The big problem is Mom never has enough change.

JULIE: *(Surprised)* Pat!

(Silence)

MRS. LOVELY: Next?

AL: What makes you our judge?

MRS. LOVELY: I'm what's called a mediator.

AL: So what do you know about judging?

MRS. LOVELY: I'm not a judge. I'm a community mediator trained by Clark County to help people settle disputes.

AL: For us?

MRS. LOVELY: Usually for parents having problems with their children. Often between victims of crime and perpetrators. Sometimes the court appoints me to mediate.

JULIE: But you run a washateria.

MRS. LOVELY: There are 120 mediators in Clark County, and all of them are trained volunteers. This is the only time I have intervened in my own behalf.

JULIE:	Does it actually work?
MRS. LOVELY:	A large percentage of the time it resolves a conflict. It also teaches people new skills for coping with a conflict. Let's go back to step two, uninterrupted presentation of the issue.
AL:	Two? What was one?
MRS. LOVELY:	Your agreement that the conflict was *our* problem, not yours or hers.
AL:	Before I tell my side of the story, I want to ask Pat something. Do you like *Popular Mechanics?*
PAT:	Yeah.
AL:	I'll bring some next week.
PAT:	All right!
AL:	Now *(Looking at* JULIE) about being a dryer hog.
MRS. LOVELY:	No name calling. Describe the problem.
AL:	I get mad when you put clothes in a dryer and go off in search of quarters. It's not fair. And your children annoy me by throwing things, spilling soap, and running all over the place.
	(Silence)
ELAINE:	There's nothing to do here.
AL:	Help your mother.
MRS. LOVELY:	Or help me fold clothes.
JULIE:	I'm so embarrassed. I'm the problem. No change, no discipline.
MRS. LOVELY:	We agreed that it's our problem.
AL:	I suppose my temper has a short fuse. I'll try to hold it in check.
PAT:	I promise to save quarters. And I won't run around spilling soaps.
ELAINE:	Me, too.
MRS. LOVELY:	All of you have worked hard at problem solving. Do we all agree that next Thursday we will work hard to avoid conflict?
JULIE:	Yes.
AL:	Agreed.
ELAINE:	I will.

PAT:	Me, too.
MRS. LOVELY:	I will, too. And I look forward to seeing you next Thursday.

Note: Mediation usually involves the use of a disinterested party who is the objective observer. There are trained mediators in many communities who have found this method of conflict resolution at least a deterrent to violence. Survey your community and inform your group about available resources. Some school districts hire trained mediators and teach mediation skills as part of social study curriculum. If you would like to start a mediation group, read *Peacemaking for Your Neighborhood* by Jennifer Beer (Philadelphia, PA: New Society Publishers, 1986).

PERSPECTIVE
A Brief Skit.

Production Notes

Characters: Lily (senior citizen), Irja (senior citizen), and Seji (teenager)
Playing time: 2 minutes
Properties: A battery or fuel powered lamp, a long table for a soup kitchen counter, aprons, salad dressing, lunch meat and/or cheese, bread, plastic bags, and knives.
Costumes: Casual clothing.
Setting: The counter of a Red Cross relief kitchen lit by a single lamp. Irja and Seji are making sandwiches, which they place in plastic bags and stack on the end of the counter.

MODERATOR:	Please welcome the I Can Survive Anything Players as they work in a Red Cross shelter kitchen.
LILY:	*(Entering left)* Who was that?
IRJA:	A National Guard colonel.
LILY:	About the power?
SEJI:	When will it be on?
IRJA:	Next week.
SEJI and LILY:	Next week?
IRJA:	They're bringing in more propane so we can keep the kitchen open.
	(SEJI pours himself a glass of milk and begins eating a sandwich.)

IRJA:	Hey! Save some for our customers. Didn't you have breakfast?
SEJI:	No. How many breakfasts did you serve?
LILY:	Around a hundred. I lost count after we ran out of eggs.
IRJA:	Well, Seji, how is the clean-up operation going at home?
SEJI:	The rugs are out, and the kitchen is emptied. Dad got the tree off the roof and covered the hole with plastic. How about your place, Lily?
LILY:	It's gone.
SEJI:	Everything?
LILY:	I've been sleeping in the church gymnasium.
SEJI:	I'm so sorry. Can I help?
IRJA:	I already offered. She's very independent, Seji. And very optimistic.
LILY:	The first day I cried. Then I looked around and got busy.
SEJI:	You're brave.
LILY:	I'm not alone. Have you noticed the way everyone behaves?
IRJA:	Dazed?
LILY:	At first. Not now. I'd call everyone peaceful.
SEJI:	I hadn't thought about it until now. Everyone stands in line patiently. There's no shoving or arguing. You're right! Absolutely no conflicts.
IRJA:	How do you account for that, Lily?
LILY:	It's perspective! They're glad to be alive.
MODERATOR:	It's important to *resolve* conflicts when they arise. However, some conflicts may be defused by viewing the issue in perspective. Defusing might be described as when one person refuses to take offense at an issue. There is biblical precedence for this. (Continue with discussion questions or divide into smaller units for discussion.)

DISCUSSION QUESTIONS

1. How does a crisis help put things into perspective? How do children view a crisis? Do adults view the same crisis the same way?
2. What does the Bible say about keeping things in perspective to avoid conflict?

3. After discussing the question, look to the Bible for guidance: Read Matthew 5:38-48. How do individuals establish a boundary line between turning the other cheek and instituting techniques for resolving conflict? How does a perspective such as the one described in the skit fit into this?

4. Read Matthew 5:9. "Peacemakers" isn't an instant state. What techniques do you use to resolve conflict? Do those techniques help you feel satisfied as a peacemaker? (Leader, see suggestions below, under Sharing Time preface by Moderator.)

5. Name some conflicts that could be avoided if we copied Jesus' role as the servant of God and servant of others.

SHARING TIME

Preface by Moderator

(Use this preface for a group without young children.) A fight on the playground is a conflict. An argument in front of the television set about which channel to watch is a conflict. A teenager's disagreement with parents over curfew time is a conflict. A disagreement between partners over business practices is a conflict. So is a long-term smoldering resentment over living arrangements for an aging parent. *A struggle or clash between ideas, beliefs, or property may be considered conflict.* This conflict may range from a small disagreement over who gets the comics from the newspaper, to who will rule a country. It may include the bully at school who socks you in the eye and two people quietly discussing how they will spend their money. The clash and struggle also may include physical abuse and emotional bondage.

Many of us are trying to discover how we can practice the love Jesus taught while avoiding the explosive violence so often found in conflict.

Good news! There are ways to resolve conflict. Some positive ways of resolving conflict are to:

a) defuse angry feelings in a humorous and constructive way.

b) distance yourself if the conflict is violent, or let an issue cool before dealing with it.

c) listen actively to get in touch with the other person's point of view.

d) apologize without saying that you are wrong or apologize when you are wrong.

e) negotiate without anger. This often leads to compromise.

f) seek help in order to prevent violence (mediation or counseling). "The Oleo Lovely Laundromat" playlet was an example of mediation. Mrs. Oleo Lovely intervened to keep the anger level from escalating.

g) develop communication skills.

h) seek immediate help if you are a victim of abuse.

Some negative ways of handling conflict are resorting to physical and mental abuse, retreating from a conflict that should have been resolved, believing that Christians should be meek and forgiving to the point of absorbing all blame for conflict, and accepting violence.

One of our challenges as Christians is to find ways to *resolve* conflict in order to keep life affirmative and balanced. Another challenge is to find ways to resolve conflict without resorting to violence. But one of the greatest challenges—a must for Christians—is reconciliation in a framework of forgiveness. For as John Wesley is reported to have said, "We may not think alike, but we can love alike."

The moderator will set the scene for small groups.

IN SMALL GROUPS

Rapport is important in order for the group to share. The group leader will introduce himself or herself and tell his or her favorite food. Ask each group member to do the same. Repeat with another request, depending on the age and mix of your group. This slow beginning is important.

Have members of the group tell briefly about conflicts they have encountered or are encountering. Elect one conflict to role play, and select participants. Avoid using the person involved in the original conflict. After the role play, discuss possible resolutions of the conflict. Vote on the most positive resolution. Role play the ending. A reluctant group might respond to a fictitious conflict between Julie, Elaine, and Pat from the skit "The Oleo Lovely Laundromat."

Repeat role plays and discussion using the positive resolution suggestions given by the moderator in the preface to the small groups section. Have fun with role play. Although this is a serious subject, it should be treated with humor. Cast roles with incongruity. For example, have a grown man play a child, or a woman play a man. Role play by necessity is exaggerated, and exaggeration is one form of humor.

CLOSING

Our hands are often barometers of our emotions. Clenched fists are an indicator of anger. Arms crossed with hands clenching arms is a defensive move that indicates a barrier between persons. A hands-on-hips stance often indicates a dare for the other person to step over the line. Practice nonthreatening hand movements, such as hands outstretched, palms up. Close with prayer.

EVENT THEME: PEACE

SCHEDULE

*Get nametags and deposit items for the needy.
*Get Together Activities:
  1. Play Boat Relay and Save Me! Save Me!
  2. Have a hot dog supper.
*Focus Activity:
  1. Perform the skit, "Pass Me a Peace of Cake."
  2. An alternate activity for an older age group is the monologue, "The Lord Give You Peace."
*Sharing Time
  1. Divide into discussion groups.
  2. Have responsive prayer and singing.

ADVANCE PREPARATION

*Publicize clothing or food drive.
*Recruit a game leader.
*Select a Moderator.
*Select a skit director and properties manager.
*Recruit discussion leaders.
*Make copies of the Responsive Prayer of Francis of Assisi (p. 50) and "Sing This Song and Celebrate" (p. 53).

ROOM ARRANGEMENT

*A table for nametags, and another table for items brought for the needy.
*A large space for games.
*Skit staging area: If no stage is available, locate stage area near a door wide enough for canoes to come through, or hide canoes behind furniture in staging area. As a last resort, use imaginary canoes.
*Arrange chairs near staging area. Later move chairs to discussion groups. Provide help for persons with handicapping conditions.

AS PEOPLE ARRIVE

*Get nametags and leave items for the needy.
*Begin games.

Boat Relay

Supplies needed: One life jacket, one paddle, and one chair for each team of ten to fifteen people.

Instructions: On each chair (which serves as a canoe) place a life jacket and a paddle. Opposite the chairs, form relay lines. Each contestant must run to the canoe chair, put on the life jacket, sit in the chair and paddle five strokes, take off the life jacket, and, leaving it with the paddle on the chair, return to the line and tag the next person, and so forth.

Save Me! Save Me!

Supplies needed: Each relay team needs a chair and a fifteen-foot rope with a loop in the end.

Instructions: Move the relay lines to about twelve feet from the chairs, closer if you have smaller children. Assign pairs within each relay line. First person runs to sit in the chair and calls "Save me! Save me!" Second person throws the rope to the drowning victim. Victim must catch the rope without getting out of the chair. Try, try again until all victims on each team have been rescued.

Note: Know your congregation. Relays are sometimes difficult for children and adults with handicapping conditions. Many handicaps are not visible. Predesignate persons responsible for helping them to become involved in the activity.

FOCUS ACTIVITY

PASS ME A PEACE OF CAKE
The shuttle driver brings peace.

Production Notes

Characters: Moderator, Nancy (eighteen years old), Tim (eight to ten years old), Mom, Uncle Bill, Granddad, and Ivan (twelve to fifteen years old).

Playing time: 8 - 10 minutes.

Properties: Four canoe paddles, two canoes, two empty rucksacks, empty water bottles, life jackets, bailing can, bakery birthday cake in a box, plastic knife, full bottle of water, and a watch in a zip-lock plastic bag.

Costumes: Nancy and Tim wear dressy casual outfits. Mom, Uncle Bill, Granddad, and Ivan wear shorts or jeans and t-shirts with tennis shoes. Mom and Uncle Bill are dripping wet as the scene begins.

Setting: A river bank with the river running across upstage. Optional shrubs and grass created from potted plants may dress the setting.

MODERATOR:	Our Down River Players present for your entertainment a playlet entitled "Pass Me a Peace of Cake." As the scene begins, four paddlers—Uncle Bill, his father, his sister, and her son, Ivan—have just completed a day long down river float trip. *(UNCLE BILL and MOM enter from stage right, drag their canoe to center back of stage, and unload gear from their canoe as they talk.)*
UNCLE BILL:	This is a great river take out point.
MOM:	It's one of the few public take out spots around.
UNCLE BILL:	Does Nancy pick you up here often?
MOM:	Four or five times a summer. *(Shakes water off the rucksack)* The water was perfect today.
UNCLE BILL:	Except at the Rock Garden, where we turned over.
MOM:	And the Meat Grinder, where our boat filled up.
UNCLE BILL:	*(Sniffs his wet shirt)* There's not much worse than wet, smelly clothes.
MOM:	I'll tell you what's worse than wet clothes—drowning.
UNCLE BILL:	Right! *(Pauses to sniff clothes again)* Oh well, Nancy should be here soon, and we can get back to the campground and change clothes. *(GRANDDAD and IVAN pull their canoe onstage next to Mom's canoe, and begin unloading their water bottle and rucksack, and bailer)*
IVAN:	Hey, Granddad! We made it!
GRANDDAD:	Without turning over!
IVAN:	*(to MOM and UNCLE BILL)* Hey! You look wet.
MOM:	Our boat filled up at the Meat Grinder.
IVAN:	I told you to lean downstream in that turn. Didn't you hear me yelling?
MOM:	Hear you? Of course I did. It was too late.
IVAN:	I've told you that every time we canoe.
MOM:	Forgive me, kid. I forget.
IVAN:	You'd better get it right. Sometime you might lean upstream and stay that way.
MOM:	I keep telling you I'm doing the best I can.
UNCLE BILL:	*(Pats her shoulder)* You were great. Don't listen to him. *(Everyone laughs and agrees.)*

GRANDDAD:	Any drinking water left?
UNCLE BILL:	Bottle's dry.
IVAN:	Ours, too.
GRANDDAD:	I'm dying of thirst.
IVAN:	Drink from the mighty Guadalupe River.
GRANDDAD:	You're kidding! I'll wait until we get back to camp. Where's Nancy? I thought she was supposed to meet us here.
MOM:	Nancy's often late. That's why I told her four instead of four-thirty.
UNCLE BILL:	What time is it now?
MOM:	*(Taking watch out of plastic bag)* Why, it's five o'clock.
IVAN:	Maybe she gave up on us and left.
MOM:	She'd never do that.
GRANDDAD:	Nancy seems awfully young to be driving that big van around. She a good driver?
IVAN:	No.
MOM:	Yes. Well, almost.
UNCLE BILL:	Is Tim safe with her?
MOM:	Don't worry, Bill. Tim's safe with Nancy. She's just . . . just . . . late.
UNCLE BILL:	*(Looks for a place to sit)* Might as well get comfortable. Here. *(Hands life jacket to Mom)* Sit on this and you won't get muddy.
	(Everyone relaxes on the ground except IVAN, *who rummages through his rucksack looking for food. He is restless and begins packing across the back of the stage in front of shrubbery.)*
IVAN:	I'm hungry.
MOM:	You're always hungry.
GRANDDAD:	He dropped his sandwich in the river.
IVAN:	*(Agitated)* I get mean when I'm hungry.
MOM:	Don't get mean with me. I'm so tired I might get grouchy, too.
IVAN:	All right. All right.
GRANDDAD:	Where can Nancy be?
UNCLE BILL:	Probably found some cute boys at the campground.

(Everyone freezes in place as the lights go dim.)

MOM:	Bill, I'm really worried about Nancy and Tim. They're two hours late.
UNCLE BILL:	I'm not worried. I'm mad. She should have more consideration for us.
IVAN:	It's your fault, Mom. You should have paid for a professional shuttle.
MOM:	Don't blame me. Get mad at Nancy.
IVAN:	I am!
GRANDDAD:	Has this happened before?
MOM:	You mean waiting for Nancy?
GRANDDAD:	Yes.
MOM:	Often.
IVAN:	Only after school in the parking lot, picking her up from the movies, after play practice, carpooling to speech contest, and three times this summer when she drove the shuttle for us.
GRANDDAD:	Don't you get angry about it?
MOM:	Of course.
UNCLE BILL:	Why don't you do something about it?
MOM:	Me?
IVAN:	Yeah, it's your car.
MOM:	But I'm glad she can drive. It's easy on me.
UNCLE BILL:	Being late is a very bad habit.
MOM:	You should know, Bill. You were late for dinner every night for years. Mom really got upset.
UNCLE BILL:	*(Stands up and paces around)* I had football practice.
MOM:	Sometimes.
GRANDDAD:	I guess we're all late sometimes.

(The sound of a door slamming is heard and footsteps come toward stage. TIM *runs onstage from stage left, followed by* NANCY.)

TIM:	They're still here!
NANCY:	Hi, everybody.

(GRANDDAD, UNCLE BILL, *and* MOM *rise and move toward* NANCY. TIM *hugs his father around the waist.)*

TIM:	Hi, Dad. *(Moves away quickly from* UNCLE BILL) Yuk! You're wet.

UNCLE BILL:	That's what you get in water.
NANCY:	She dunk someone in the Meat Grinder again?
MOM:	Right.
IVAN:	*(Angry)* You're late.
NANCY:	A little.
IVAN:	An hour and a half!
NANCY:	That late?
TIM:	We had a flat tire and I helped fix it.
MOM:	You changed a tire?
NANCY:	Some guys stopped and helped us.
UNCLE BILL:	I told you she'd find some cute guys.
IVAN:	An hour and a half to fix a tire?
TIM:	Well, we had to stand in line at the bakery.
MOM:	Nancy, you've got to be more considerate.
GRANDDAD:	You knew what time to be here.
NANCY:	I did the best I could.
IVAN:	We nearly starved waiting for you.
NANCY:	*(Raising voice)* Last time I waited on you for an hour.
IVAN:	That was different. We helped rescue someone on the river.
NANCY:	*(Getting angry)* What about two months ago when I sat in this exact spot waiting for you two hours until it got dark?
IVAN:	You weren't hungry and thirsty.
	(GRANDDAD waves his arms in the air as if to stop the argument. The argument goes on.)
NANCY:	*(Yelling)* What has that got to do with it? I waited!
IVAN:	Yeah! Listening to the radio and eating popcorn.
GRANDDAD:	*(Yells, still holding arms in the air.)* Quiet!
	(There is sudden silence)
GRANDDAD:	Was anyone late to be mean or get even with anyone?
NANCY, IVAN, and MOM:	No!
GRANDDAD:	Then let's make peace.

	(Thoughtful silence)
MOM:	Okay.
GRANDDAD:	I don't mean forget it. I mean, let's mediate.
IVAN:	What's that?
GRANDDAD:	Give, take, decide. Was anyone hurt by having to wait?
MOM, IVAN, and NANCY:	No.
GRANDDAD:	Was anyone mad afterward?
NANCY:	Yes.
MOM:	No.
IVAN:	Yes.
GRANDDAD:	We need a rule of the river.
IVAN:	What's that?
GRANDDAD:	The persons who get here first won't get mad. Just say, "They're doing the best they can."
MOM:	But we all have to be considerate.
GRANDDAD:	That's the key. No one deliberately keeps someone waiting. Okay?
MOM:	Okay.
NANCY:	Okay.
IVAN:	Maybe.
GRANDDAD:	Has to be unanimous for it to work.
MOM:	This would make peace in the school parking lot and after the movies, too. Consideration might make peace. And forgiveness . . . it's fixing the problem, not fixing the blame.
IVAN:	Maybe. I'll think about it. But I'm starving. What did you get at the bakery?
	(TIM runs offstage, returns carrying a boxed birthday cake with a bottle of water tucked under one arm.)
TIM:	We brought Granddad a birthday cake since he wasn't visiting on his birthday.
	(NANCY opens the box and takes out the cake while TIM opens the bottle of water.)
GRANDDAD:	It's beautiful. You were very thoughtful to do this.

NANCY:	You're not mad that I was late because of getting it?
MOM:	No.

(NANCY looks at IVAN, waiting for an answer, but he is silent. TIM gives IVAN a drink from the water bottle.)

GRANDDAD:	Let's call it the peace cake. Everyone who eats a piece will remember the rule of the river. If you're waiting for someone, don't hold it against them. Think peaceful thoughts.
IVAN:	*(Grouchy)* We don't even have a knife.
NANCY:	*(Pulling a plastic knife from her pocket)* The lady at the bakery gave me one. *(Hands knife to GRANDDAD)*
GRANDDAD:	*(Cuts cake)* Chocolate! My favorite!

(NANCY, TIM, and UNCLE BILL crowd around GRANDDAD, each receiving a piece of cake. IVAN stays away from the group while the others eat cake and drink from the bottle.)

GRANDDAD:	Delicious.
NANCY:	Good.
TIM:	Happy birthday, Granddad.
GRANDDAD:	Thanks, Tim. *(Drinks)* The water is really good. Thanks.
MOM:	*(to IVAN)* Do you remember the word *reconciliation?*
IVAN:	I've heard it.
MOM:	It means forgive in love and make things right.
NANCY:	I'm sorry I made you wait, Ivan.
IVAN:	That's okay, Nancy.
NANCY:	Well then, eat some of Granddad's peace cake.
IVAN:	Oh, all right. Pass me a PEACE of cake.

(NANCY hands IVAN a piece of cake, which he eats while the rest sing "Happy Birthday" to GRANDDAD.)

IVAN:	Happy birthday, peace.

SMALL GROUPS

The leader should have each person in the group tell his or her name and favorite water sport. If you have young children in your group, play charades (act out and guess action) of "Conflicts or Troubles in My Life." Group leader goes first. Were there similarities? What was the Rule of the River? How can the Rule of the River help resolve conflict? Make a group list of places where the rule might apply. You may need to suggest that some conflicts need discussion at family council, mediation with a third party, or counseling. For groups with older participants you may want to use the following questions:

1. When or where do you have to wait for someone? How do you feel about it?
2. In the skit, what was the Rule of the River?
3. Name instances of conflict or nonpeace in your life or the lives of those around you. How could applying the Rule of the River help? (Be ready to say that some conflicts are so complicated they need a different kind of help. Look for volatile situations in your group. For information on mediation, see Event Theme: Resolving Conflict, p. 30.)
4. Ask group members to share their techniques for reducing conflict and restoring peace. Focus on fixing the problem, not the blame. (Churches need to be aware of potential violence or abuse in their congregations. If you as group leader sense this, report it to your pastor or other appropriate person.)

CLOSING

At a signal, groups cease discussion and the moderator closes the session. If you have not used "Sing This Song and Celebrate" before, have it sung as a solo. Close with the responsive prayer below.

Responsive Prayer of Francis of Assisi

MODERATOR: Lord, make me an instrument of thy peace.

GROUP: Where there is hatred, let me sow love.

MODERATOR: Lord, make me an instrument of thy peace.

GROUP: Where there is injury, help me sow pardon; where there is doubt, faith.

MODERATOR: Lord, make me an instrument of thy peace.

GROUP: Where there is despair, let me sow hope. Where there is sadness, let me sow joy.

MODERATOR: Lord, make me an instrument of thy peace.

GROUP: Where there is darkness, let me be aware that light is possible and do something about it.

MODERATOR: O Divine Master, grant that I may not so much seek to be consoled, as to console; not so much to be understood, as to understand; not so much to be loved as to love.

GROUP and MODERATOR: For it is in giving that we receive. It is in pardoning that we are pardoned. It is in dying that we are born again to eternal life. Amen.

ALTERNATE ACTIVITY

THE LORD GIVE YOU PEACE
A monologue of Francis of Assisi.

(FRANCIS sits center stage at a table, barefooted, dressed only in a worn tunic with a tattered surplice shaped in the sign of the cross. A dingy rag is tucked into a rope belt around his waist. On the table in front of FRANCIS are a wooden bowl, wooden spoon, and a clay or gourd cup. A similar setting for the imaginary BERNARD is across the table from him. As they eat, FRANCIS tells his story to BERNARD, a recent convert. FRANCIS is lost in his own thoughts as he begins.)

I was only twenty with stardust in my eyes when I rode off to war. I wasn't a peacemaker then, only a boy dreaming of becoming a knight. What? *(Pause)* You don't like the food? Oh. I'll explain it to you one more time, Bernard. This is our only food because I gave the rest of it to Leone's family. We can't serve the poor and be superior to them. You'll learn that when you have been with us longer. Come on, eat up. *(Bows head for a silent prayer)* The Lord give you peace. *(Tastes food)* Ugh! You're right! It tastes worse than the food in the Perugian jail. Only being from a rich family saved my life. Even then the food tasted like pig slop. *(Tastes again)* In that jail, I saw so much pain and hunger, that I was never the same. I discovered that the poor, ugly wretches who made me sick to my stomach were . . . well . . . were children of God. *(Tastes food again)* When I got out of jail, my rich friends appeared again, and we once again started our parties and drinking. But it wasn't fun anymore.

Do you know, Bernard, that compassion isn't a feeling? It's an action! That idea overtook me one day as a leper walked toward me with his hand outstretched for alms. I was so overcome by his plight that I pressed coins into his deformed hand and kissed his fingers. Then I was sick with loathing. Strange though, a feeling of peace so overcame me that I grabbed him and hugged him. *(Pauses to look heavenward)* My act of humility became a true moment of conversion. "He who possesses humility finds grace with God, and perfect peace with his neighbor."*

(FRANCIS rises, takes the rag from his belt, and begins to wipe his bowl, and continues to clean both his dishes and those of BERNARD as he speaks.)

After that I gave to the dirty, smelly poor people. Father was so rich I thought he wouldn't miss some of *his* rolls of cloth and *his* horse I sold to get money for the poor. He missed them all right! Mad! You've never seen anyone so mad. Beat me and locked me in a dark cell. While I sat there I argued back and forth with myself over stealing versus the injustices to the poor. I enjoyed being rich. But hadn't I been praying that God would direct me to my mission? Of course I had. God wanted me to help the poor. Yet, I was covered with guilt for going against my father.

*Quoted from *The Little Flowers of St. Francis,* trans. Dom. Roger Hudelston, London, 1953, and found in *Christian Ethics,* Waldo Beach and Richard Niebuhr (New York: Ronald Press Co.), p. 165.

(Slowly, almost absentmindedly wipes a cup again and again) What happened next, Bernard? Oh, an angel, my mother, turned me loose from that awful room. But Father had me arrested, and there was the public humiliation of a trial. Finally, I returned the money. *(Rubs cup faster and faster)* Then right there in public I took off my clothes and threw them at my father's feet. The bishop's gardener gave me this old worn tunic. *(Yanks at the tunic)* Ah, . . . well, enough history. There, see, now I've cleaned your dishes for you. *(Gestures toward table. Bows to* BERNARD*)* The Lord give you peace. *(Pause)* And you. *(Rises and stacks utensils on the end of the table during dialogue)* People think you're a nut if you *want* to be poor. But I became a poor nut wandering around helping the unfortunate. When I greeted them with "The Lord give you peace" they eventually talked to me. I tried to imitate Christ—an impossible job—but I tried, and still try.

I preach peace. There should be peace with God brought by keeping the Ten Commandments. And, any Christian should try to get along with others by following Jesus' teachings. This makes for peace in relationships. You've heard me announce the gospel of peace and conversion. But you and all the brothers who have followed me have been pelted with garbage, denied food and places to sleep. We have slept in caves and on church porches. Yet we must be patient in trouble, forgiving of those who don't understand. *(Looks to exit)* Wait, Bernard, don't leave me talking to myself. We must bless those who persecute us. Our Lord tells us to pray for them. "Prayer is the beginning, the middle, and the end of all good; prayer illuminates the soul and enables it to discern between good and evil."* After prayer, we have much urgent work to do. It is a weight on my shoulders. But I'll tell you a secret, Bernard. The joy of this work swells up inside me and gives glow to my whole being. I love it!

*(*FRANCIS *walks away from the table, turns, facing* BERNARD *at the door, bows to him)*

The Lord give you peace, Bernard. *(Exits stage left)*

INFORMATION AND DISCUSSION

Francis of Assisi, who lived from 1182 to 1226, was aware that in his lifetime the churches were wealthy and beset by sects and heresies and tended to ignore the poor and homeless, while catering to the wealthy aristocracy and tradespeople. Francis was not against the church, but chose to imitate Christ in simplicity. He founded the Franciscan order whose four main qualities were humility, simplicity, poverty, and prayer. Another order for women, Poor Clares, was founded by one of his followers. The decision by Francis to preach peace and conversion, and to totally give up his life of luxury in favor of poverty, was a painful one that he came to through discovering God in stages. He had to look for peace within himself, and found it only when he learned to serve others in ways that he thought imitated Christ.

*Quoted from *The Little Flowers of St. Francis,* trans. Dom. Roger Hudelston, London, 1953, and found in *Christian Ethics,* Waldo Beach and Richard Niebuhr (New York: Ronald Press Co.), p. 170.

1. If we decided to practice humility in our lives, how would we need to change?
2. How can we simplify our lives and our life-styles?
3. If you recall the life-style of Jesus and his followers and the life-style of Francis of Assisi, what changes might you need to make in the way you spend your money? The way you spend your time?
4. All of us cannot sell or give away our possessions and travel around barefooted, but we can become more aware of the needs of others. Make a list of unmet needs your group sees in the immediate community. What can you do about these needs?
5. Read together the Responsive Prayer of Francis of Assisi. Individually, with pencil and paper, list ways you can sow love, pardon, hope, joy, and light. Be specific. Where in your life can you be more consoling, understanding, loving, giving?
6. How was Francis of Assisi a peacemaker?

Close by reading the responsive prayer of Francis of Assisi.

Sing "Sing This Song and Celebrate."

Sing This Song and Celebrate

(for Katharine Sumner Cook)

Words and Music by Jerry O. Cook

Introduction

Chorus

C F G7   C   G

mf ——————— *f*   Sing this song and cel - e - brate   the

C   F   C   G

life that God has giv-en you!__ Praise the Lord and cel-e-brate with

(first three times)   *(last time)*

C   F   C   C   F   C

joy for - ev -er new! __   1. And joy for-ev-er new! __
                           2. And
                           3. And

Verses

F   G   C   Am

God   will   grant you   the   gift   of   love   And
God   will   grant you   the   gift   of   peace, So
God   will   grant you   the   gift   of   life,   So

F   G   C   Am

show   you   how   to   share, _____   So
you   may   al - ways stand— _____ Se -
you   may   al - ways be _____   A

F   G   C   Am

you   may be blessed all the days of your life,   By
cure____ and safe____ and un - a - fraid,   Up -
child of the world and a   child of the Lord— Through

F   G   C   F   G7

friends who love and care!
held   by   God's own hand!
faith   a - live and free!

EVENT THEME:
IT'S ALL RIGHT TO BE DIFFERENT

Schedule

*Get Together Activities:
   1. Get nametags.
   2. Learn at Alike but Different Playground (optional games).
   3. Have a potluck meal.
*Focus Activity:
   1. "Marooned!" (differences)
   2. "May I Come Play?" (prejudice or differences)
   3. "Handicapped to Cheeseburger" (handicapping conditions)
*Sharing
   1. Small Groups
*Closing:
   1. Reader's theater, "Yeah, God!"
   2. Optional: The children's choir may sing "Clap Your Hands Together."

ADVANCE PREPARATION

*Make nametags with the caption "God's Child."
*Select a leader and collect the following materials for Alike but Different Playground: blindfolds, canes, wheelchairs, crutches, tape measures, large print *Upper Room* or other large print devotional material, foreign language reading materials, braille letters or books, mirrors, spectacles, magnifying glasses, and telephone books. If you have chosen to emphasize racial prejudice during this event, add ethnic items such as foods or costumes and books printed in several languages. Have an interpreter present. Place an old sheet on a tension curtain rod hung in a doorway. Cut a hole in the curtain large enough for a nose to poke through. Place a stepping stool behind the curtain for children. Send six people behind the curtain who will poke their noses through the hole. Those gathered on the opposite side of the curtain are to guess whose nose is showing. This exercise is designed to show differences and similarities.
*Select the drama or dramas that reflect the emphasis you have chosen for this event.

*Recruit a drama director and song leader or musical group.
*Select a moderator. At the meal, have the moderator compare a pot luck meal to racial, cultural, and physical differences in our society.
*Recruit and train leaders for small groups. You will need Bibles for these groups.

ROOM ARRANGEMENT

*A table for nametags.
*Set aside an area for the Alike but Different Playground that is large enough for everyone to try the wheelchairs and crutches, and so forth. Books will need a table and chairs. Put paper on the wall near the tape measure and encourage everyone to mark his or her height by drawing a line and writing his or her name.
*Plan an area for staging drama or dramas. "May I Come Play" works best if the person playing Roman is not visible.

AS PEOPLE ARRIVE

*Make nametags. Moderator directs people to take pot luck food to dining room and then to go to the Alike but Different Playground. At the playground, the leader encourages people to play, ask questions, and pretend handicaps as they use the equipment. Line up an audience for Guess Whose Nose.

FOCUS ACTIVITIES

MAROONED
A monologue about prejudice.

Production Notes

Character: Anyman (or Anywoman), event Moderator
Playing time: 1 minute
Properties: Comb, two nuts.
Costumes: Anyman (or Anywoman), anything appropriate for a person marooned on a desert island for a month, such as tattered clothing and no shoes.

MODERATOR: Our Potluck Player tonight is _____, who portrays Anyman (or Anywoman), who has been marooned on a Pacific island for a month.

(ANYMAN *walks to stage center, looks right and left. He shields his eyes from the sun and scans the horizon. He speaks in a slow, listless manner, getting enthusiastic only at the prospect of each rescue.*)

ANYMAN: I've been stranded on my own little island so long I'm dying of loneliness. I talk to myself, and even I am boring. Once a row boat came within shouting distance, but the three people in the boat weren't my skin color. I didn't trust them. *(Pauses to comb tangles from hair)* One morning I got very excited when a yacht anchored off shore. I swam out that way as fast as I could, but when I got close, I saw two old men and an old woman. I mean really old and wrinkled, probably senile. Well, I couldn't get involved with someone like that. I swam back to the safety of my island. *(Cracks one nut against another)* Then one night I saw a cruise ship coming. It was beautiful with its little sparkling lights around the deck. I built a big bonfire and shouted "Help! Help!" As it got closer, though, the rock music was so loud I could barely hear the laughing and carrying on. I suppose it was a wild teenage party cruise. I stomped out my signal fire—definitely not my kind of people. God knows I'm lonesome. He will send my kind of people to rescue me. I wish he would hurry. I'm lonely.

MODERATOR: *(leading applause)* An island can be anywhere—a table at school, the coffee cart at the office, a committee meeting at the church, a scaffolding at work, or a neighborhood where people don't talk to each other.

If your group is large, break into discussion groups.

DISCUSSION QUESTIONS

1. Which rescue should Anyman have taken? Why?
2. How do you feel about persons with skin of another color? About older persons? About partying teenagers? Do you feel the same about groups of people who are other colors or old, or teenagers as groups?
3. What did you learn about Anyman from his actions? What were his attitudes toward life, himself, others, God?
4. What advice can you give Anyman?

MAY I COME UP TO PLAY?
A quick skit on differences.

Production Notes

Characters: Moderator, Geraldine, Brett, Kate, Roman (male), all children who may be played by adults.
Playing time: 1½ minutes.
Setting and Properties: The scene is a treehouse furnished with a low table and play dishes. Roman is out of sight offstage.

Costumes: Clothing appropriate for children.

MODERATOR:	Our After Potluck Players bring us a scene from the neighborhood tree house.
GERALDINE:	I get to be the mother.
BRETT:	No, Geraldine, you were the mother yesterday.
GERALDINE:	Well, I'm going to be the mother again today. And that's final.
BRETT:	Okay. But today the father decides what we eat.
GERALDINE:	Well, this is already pretend steak.
BRETT:	And this is pretend french fries. I hate baked potatoes with steak.
	(Enter KATE)
GERALDINE:	Hi, Kate. You have to be baby brother.
KATE:	I want to be mother.
GERALDINE:	*I'm* mother.
KATE:	*(Sits on floor)* Then you have to feed me.
ROMAN:	*(Calling from offstage)* Hey! Up there! May I come up and play?
GERALDINE and BRETT:	Shh. It's Roman.
ROMAN:	Hey! I said may I come up and play?
GERALDINE:	There's no more room.
ROMAN:	Yes, there is.
GERALDINE:	Wait a minute.
KATE:	*(In stage whisper)* Why can't he come up?
GERALDINE:	*(Not softly)* He's different.
KATE:	*(Softly)* How?
GERALDINE:	Well *(Pause)* you know, he's . . . he's . . . well, just different.
KATE:	So?
GERALDINE:	Well, I don't want to play with anyone who's different.
KATE:	Why?
GERALDINE:	My mom said not to.
KATE:	But we're all different.
GERALDINE:	Not that different.

KATE: I think we should let Roman come up. He could be Uncle
                   George visiting.

GERALDINE: I said no! And it's my treehouse!

ROMAN: May I come up?

GERALDINE: No. There isn't room.

ROMAN: (Despondent) Oh.

KATE: Wait a minute, Roman. I'll come down.

Moderator leads applause. If your group is small, continue with
discussion. Divide a large group into smaller sections for discussion.

DISCUSSION QUESTIONS

1. What came to you mind when Geraldine said, "He's different"? Why do
   you think that difference came to your mind?
2. What kinds of differences do you encounter at school? In the
   workplace? On the bus? At church? If you do not notice any
   differences, it is possible that you have created an environment for
   yourself that is "my kind of people." Or perhaps you are unconsciously
   screening out those who are different. Think again.
3. (This question is for an older group.) Prejudices are built into our
   culture by advertising, myths, our families, and by the way we label
   things. For example, "flesh" colored crayons are pink and "nude"
   colored pantyhose are white. Name some ways these and other
   prejudices are built into our culture and programmed into our
   thinking.
4. What is prejudice?
5. Why do we like to feel superior to someone or a group of persons?
6. Brett was a silent voice in the "He's different" discussion. What did he
   say by his silence?
7. How may we overcome our feelings that some persons are better and
   others are worse?

Suggestion: We may admit that there are differences and celebrate the
rich world of differences. We may develop our own self-esteem while
teaching ourselves that people are different but of equal value. We may look
for common experiences and values. (These suggestions are from the
pamphlet *A New Look at Prejudice, Program Implications for Educational
Organizations* by Helen Foss, The National Conference of Christians and
Jews, 71 Fifth Avenue, New York, New York 10003, 1986. Other pamphlets
are available with more ideas.)

HANDICAPPED TO CHEESEBURGER
A monologue.

Production Notes

Characters: Jeff Martin, junior high student; Moderator.
Playing time: 1½ minutes
Properties: Book bag, ball, medic alert tag, and a bench.
Costume: Jeff wears school clothes, a Medic Alert tag around his neck, and has a book bag slung over his shoulder. He *quietly* bounces a soft (quiet) ball during the monologue.

MODERATOR: Our Potluck Player, is _____, who portrays Jeff Martin waiting for someone in front of his school.

(JEFF *enters the stage, bouncing a ball. He stops bouncing, removes his book bag, and places it on the bench.)*

JEFF: Yesterday, right here, I saw a kid on crutches drop his books. When I bent down to pick them up, I saw heavy metal braces on his legs. I don't know why, but I looked away. I wondered how he could walk with those heavy things on his legs. He thanked me for picking up his books. *(Opens book bag and takes out book)* I left feeling thankful that my handicap doesn't show. I have needlemarks everywhere from taking insulin shots. Except for the Medic Alert tag around my neck, no one knows about my diabetes. *(Puts down book and bounces the ball)* As I walked home, I got to thinking about all the kids in my class who have handicaps. There's Brian who lost all his hair because of chemical treatments for leukemia. He wears a funny orange cap. Calls it Harry, you know, for instead of hair. *(Bounces ball)* I tried to remember the names of three kids in my grade who have speech problems. They have a hard time making book reports and answering questions in class. I wonder why they can't talk like the rest of us. *(Bounces call)* Then there's Alice and Jane. We call them Old Iron Bones because they wear back and neck braces. I wonder what caused their bones to go crooked. They work in the library instead of taking PE. Man! I wish I could do that, but Dad's a doctor, and he says exercise is good for diabetics. *(Sits on bench and scans the horizon as if looking for someone)* After supper last night I told my dad about the people with handicaps I had seen. He said thousands of people struggle against disabilities that people can't see. Like the girl who makes her letters backward, the hyperactive boy who can't sit still, and the kids with hearing aids or glasses. There are even kids too afraid or too sick to go to school. They have special teachers come to their houses. *(Walks around the bench, scanning the horizon)* Dad says a handicap is when a person has something that bothers him or her so much that normal activity is hard. Like you have to take extra time reading or walking, or have to have special teachers. I told him I'm curious about handicaps. He said that was okay, but not all people want to talk about their problems. When I told him about the kid on crutches and asked him if I should offer to help, he gave me an answer that made sense. *(Sits down, bouncing ball from sitting position)* I should have thought of it myself. He said, "Remind yourself that persons with handicaps have names and talents and likes and dislikes. You can probably help most by being friendly." He said to find out if they are persons I enjoy being with. *(Stands up and walks around the bench)* That's why I'm hanging around here. I wonder what kind of music the kid on crutches likes. And does he like cheeseburgers? I hope so. I know where to get great cheeseburgers and fries. *(Waves hand to stage left and calls)* Hi! Wait a minute!

DISCUSSION QUESTIONS

1. Review the monologue's definition of handicapping conditions. With this in mind, name as many handicapping conditions as you can, and write them on paper. How many of these are visible?
2. When you meet someone, do you know if he or she has a handicapping condition?
3. What kind of general attitude toward other people will help you be considerate of persons with handicapping conditions? (Such as patience, valuing each person individually, and acting out of love.)
4. In many instances, persons with handicaps are looked up to as inspirations to others. Imagine that you have a handicap. What kind of strain would this be to your personality? Would you like to be valued because of an accomplishment such as playing the piano? According to the skit, what is a healthy attitude toward a person with a handicap?
5. Name some ways a person with a handicap may be seen as a person rather than an illness.
6. As a person, what is the best way to relate to a person with a handicapping condition?
7. Think of a person with a handicapping condition whom you know. What do you know about that person? Does what you think of relate to the condition, or the person behind that condition? Is this someone you wish to know more about? Please don't rush out and start asking persons with handicapping conditions questions about themselves, but

if this person is in your workplace or classroom and you have a natural occasion for talking to him or her, share yourself and try to get past the barrier you may have felt about the condition. Be person to person. In this group, discuss the difficulties you might encounter. Share success stories.

8. As a church, how are the following needs recognized and met:

a. Physical needs: Classrooms for the deaf and/or persons with learning disabilities or parking spaces for persons with a mobility impairment?

b. Spiritual needs: Interpreters for the deaf at worship and other meetings, hearing aids, instruction at the level of need, inclusion in prayer and study groups, and attitudes by the clergy, church staff, and volunteer leaders that lead the congregation to this inclusion?

c. Fellowship needs: Activities where people with handicapping conditions may be involved with other persons, inclusion in the work of the church—such as teaching and committee work, and opportunities for recreation with all persons?

d. Planning needs: Inclusion on building committees and other groups doing the planning for educational and physical facilities, and care group planning to help meet the needs of persons with handicaps.

CLOSING

Optional: Have children's choir sing "Clap Your Hands Together" by Bob Burroughs, available from Broadman Press, Nashville, Tennessee.

YEAH, GOD!
A reader's theater.

MODERATOR: There should be no barriers to group worship. Acknowledging our differences as God's children means that we plan for each other in the ways we worship. Educational or cultural differences, language, or physically handicapping conditions need not be barriers to worshiping God. Everyone can respond to God in some way. The following reader's theater is written to help each of us become more aware of the limitations placed on others. *(Instructions to the readers: Notice that the reading is divided into thought clusters, each having three sentences. A slight pause between each cluster will give the audience time to change visualizations. Practice the rhythm of threes.)*

READER 1: Sing Yeah! Yeah! God.

READER 2: Praise him with your signing if you cannot speak.

READER 3: Praise him with your humming if the words aren't your language.

READER 1: Praise him with your clapping.

READER 2: Praise him with your stomping if you have no hands.

READER 3:   Praise him with your hissing if you have no feet.

READER 1:   Praise him with your musical instrument.

READER 2:   Praise him with your rattling if you cannot play.

READER 3:   Praise him with any joyful sound.

READER 1:   Praise him with dance.

READER 2:   Praise him with mime if you cannot dance.

READER 3:   Praise him with any part of you that will move.

READER 1:   Praise him with your Bible reading.

READER 2:   Praise him with your listening if you cannot read.

READER 3:   Praise him with colored cloth and flowers.

**READERS 1,
2, and 3:**   Respond to God with joy! Praise him!

With a little advance planning "Yeah, God!" may be adapted for audience participation. Use only one reader, who will instruct the audience to follow each statement with an enactment of that suggestion. Have someone ready with a Bible and brightly colored cloth and flowers.

EVENT THEME: PRAYER AND PRETZELS

This event becomes adaptable to a weekend retreat by using a drama and discussion questions and activities separately.

SCHEDULE

*Get nametags.
*Get Together Activity:
  1. Make pretzels.
  2. Assemble for skits while pretzels cool.
*Focus Activity:
  1. Skits to be presented in order:
    "Singing in the Shower"
    "Bernice Talks"
    "The Album"

*Sharing Time
  1. Divide into groups to eat pretzels and talk about prayer.
  2. Say closing prayer. Take pretzel recipe home.
  3. Option: Make a family blessing tri-fold.

ADVANCE PREPARATION

*Recruit table captains for pretzel making, and make copies of the pretzel recipe. Arrange for ovens or reserve kitchen. Table captains may serve as group discussion leaders.
*Select a drama director to recruit casts and rehearse brief dramas. (See introduction p. 5).
*If you select the alternate activity, collect supplies for making blessing prayer tri-fold.

ROOM ARRANGEMENT

*Place a table at the door for nametags.
*If the group is small, meet in the kitchen for pretzel making. Otherwise, set up tables accommodating six to eight persons. On each table place a toaster

oven, pretzel dough that has been made in advance, a knife, baking tins of appropriate size, potholders, and handwashing and drying materials.
*Place chairs around the staging area which has been set by a door.

AS PEOPLE ARRIVE

*Make nametags.
*Moderator directs persons to pretzel making tables.

FOCUS ACTIVITY

Pretzel is derived from the Latin word *pretiola,* which means "a small reward." The story is told that an Italian monk some fifteen hundred years ago taught prayers to children. He gave them rewards of small pretzels shaped in the form of arms folded in prayer.

Twisting pretzels has since become an activity of intercessory prayer. When you twist a pretzel say a prayer for someone. During this twisting time it may be possible to talk about what happens when we pray for others. Francis of Assisi said, "The gift of prayer is no small gift, to whomever it is given." It is a gift implying love, thoughtfulness, and often action on the part of the person who says the prayer.

PRETZEL MAKING DIRECTIONS

Children love to make pretzels, but *be careful that they do not get burned on the oven.*

Use the following pretzel recipe, or buy cans of soft breadsticks from the grocer's dairy case. These will be larger and will take more space and time to cook. Experiment with them at home.

Prayer Pretzels

1 package dry yeast
1½ cups lukewarm water (not hot)
2 Tablespoons sugar
1 teaspoon salt
4 cups flour
1 beaten egg
salt

Dissolve yeast in warm water and let rise a few minutes. Add sugar and salt and blend in 4 cups flour. Turn dough out on floured table or bread board and knead until smooth. Refrigerate until you are ready to use at your table.

At your table you will need the following supplies: Egg, egg beater, bowl, sharp knife, pastry brush, salt, timer, wet towel, paper towels, dusting flour for table top, spatula, cooling rack, potholders.

Preheat oven to 325 degrees. Lightly grease cookie sheet or toaster oven tray. Cut off four-inch pieces of dough, roll into ropes about six to eight inches, or a length you can easily twist. Twist into shape with loop at top and two arms folded over. Arrange on lightly greased toaster oven tray, allowing space between pretzels for expansion. Brush with beaten egg—those places you miss will not brown. Sprinkle with salt. Bake 12-15 minutes. Toaster ovens vary, so check after 7-8 minutes.

NEXT STEPS IN THINKING ABOUT PRAYER

Two skits and a dialogue will help participants focus on prayer questions and answers. Present them in order so that they show morning, daytime, and evening.

Begin first skit only after pretzel makers have finished and cleaned up, including handwashing. Table captains may need to remain with the ovens to complete baking. Sing familiar fun songs as persons gather.

DRAMA 1: SINGING IN THE SHOWER
A skit about the time and definition of prayer.

Production Notes

Characters: Barbara (teenager), Cousin Jim (twenty years old), Tom (eight to ten years old), Mom, Moderator.

Playing time: 4 minutes.

Properties: Four towels, four toothbrushes, four tubes of toothpaste, a door to stage right or left which represents the bathroom door.

Costumes: All wear pajamas, bathrobes, and bedroom slippers.

Setting: The hallway outside the Preston family bathroom.

MODERATOR:	We present the Early Morning Players in their quest for a quick shower. The scene is the Preston family hallway, early morning, where Tom, Mom, and visiting Cousin Jim wait by the bathroom door. Barbara Preston is in the bathroom.
	(COUSIN JIM, TOM, *and* MOM *are clustered outside the bathroom door. If your door is by necessity at back of staging area, take care that characters stand facing or profile to the audience.*)
BARBARA:	(*Singing*) Singing in the shower. Singing la, la, la. Joy, joy, joy. La, te, da, la, la.
COUSIN JIM:	(*Yelling*) Hurry up, Barbara. This isn't Carnegie Hall.
BARBARA:	(*Calling loudly*) I'm hurrying.
TOM:	Your time is up in one minute.
BARBARA:	(*Singing*) Jesus loves me this I know, for the Bible tells me so.

MOM:	*(Calling)* Barbara, hurry. Cousin Jim has an appointment at the employment office. *(Yelling)* It's important!
BARBARA:	*(Yelling)* So is this. *(Softer, but audible)* Okay, God. I have to make it short today. Thanks for the great day.
TOM:	*(To* MOM *and* COUSIN JIM*)* Who's she talking to?
MOM:	No one else in there.
COUSIN JIM:	Sounded like she said God.
BARBARA:	*(Continuing softly while voices talk over hers)* This is a big day for me. I need you today. Please help me to remember to be kind and unselfish today, and help me remember not to gossip. *(*COUSIN JIM *begins his talk.* BARBARA *continues.)* Or maybe I should say help me look for good in other people so I'll say good things.
COUSIN JIM:	I really need this job. The appointment was hard to get.
TOM:	What's the job appointment?
COUSIN JIM:	Computer analyst.
MOM:	If this one doesn't come through, remember you're always welcome here.
TOM:	*(Yelling)* If you're not out in thirty seconds, Cousin Jim is coming in.
BARBARA:	*(Calling)* All right! All right! *(Softly, but audibly)* And be with Cousin Jim as he looks for a job. Help him find strength and power.
COUSIN JIM:	*(Hand on doorknob)* I'm coming in.
	(The door opens, and BARBARA *stands there in her robe with a towel wrapped around her head.)*
TOM:	What took you so long?
BARBARA:	I prayed while I showered.
TOM:	We have a guest who's in a hurry. Can't you pray on your own time?
BARBARA:	I prayed for you, Cousin Jim. I asked God to make you strong.
MOM:	Bathroom prayer is new for us. I'm surprised.
BARBARA:	Our Bible study group is trying something new. We all agreed to tie our prayer to an act we do every day as a way of remembering to pray.
COUSIN JIM:	Thanks for the prayer. *(Exits behind door)*
TOM:	*(To* MOM*)* You go next, Mom, so you can cook breakfast.
BARBARA:	I'll cook breakfast.

TOM:	The world's coming to an end!
BARBARA:	Not likely.
MOM:	What brought this on?
BARBARA:	Last week I discovered I had been using God as a Santa Claus—gimme this, gimme that—gimme, gimme. I found out that prayer changes the person who prays, and that God helps more than he gives. And I want to help you.
MOM:	Great discovery.
TOM:	*(Yelling)* Hurry up, Cousin Jim.
BARBARA:	Be sure to tell Cousin Jim what I said about prayer. *(Exits stage left)*
TOM:	*(Calling after* BARBARA*)* You tell him after breakfast. That is if your cooking doesn't kill him.

DRAMA 2: BERNICE TALKS
A dialogue about prayer in action.

Production Notes

Characters: Bernice (elderly), Ashley (twenty-five), Moderator.
Playing time: 4 minutes
Properties: Two telephones, a rocking chair, a small table, books, an exercise mat, and a red bandana.
Costumes: Bernice wears casual clothing suitable for a woman over sixty who does not leave the house often. Ashley wears a jogging suit and tights, or shorts and a shirt.
Setting: The dialogue occurs by telephone with Bernice, stage right, in the living room of her upstairs apartment. She sits facing the audience in a rocking chair. A small table next to her holds some books, the telephone, and a red bandana. Stage left, Ashley, holding the phone, sits on an exercise mat. She faces stage right.

MODERATOR:	The Mid-Morning Players bring you a scene from Dial-A-Friend, a community program designed to help persons living alone make daily contact with someone in the community. Ashley talks to Bernice, who lives several blocks away in an upstairs apartment.
BERNICE:	*(Picks up phone)* Hello.
ASHLEY:	Bernice! I'm so glad you finally answered. This is Ashley.
BERNICE:	I know.
ASHLEY:	I was worried about you when you didn't answer.

BERNICE:	I've been wondering about you, too. I heard sirens over your way last night. You all right?
ASHLEY:	Yes. That was just a smoky electrical fire at the supermarket next door.
BERNICE:	Lots of noise! I worried that you were in trouble.
ASHLEY:	Talk about trouble. Did you hear the gang fight on your street yesterday?
BERNICE:	Oh, that. It was just a rumble.
ASHLEY:	A rumble? Bernice you sound like you might belong to one of the gangs.
BERNICE:	No, but I watched them. One group rode motorcycles and wore red bandanas and black jeans.
ASHLEY:	What about the other gang, the Raiders?
BERNICE:	Just a bunch of kids carrying chains.
ASHLEY:	And knives?
BERNICE:	Couldn't tell from up here. My eyesight isn't too good.
ASHLEY:	You mean they fought right under your window?
BERNICE:	In the street.
ASHLEY:	What did you do?
BERNICE:	*(Picks up red bandanna from table)* I put on my bandana.
ASHLEY:	*(Stands up)* You *didn't?*
BERNICE:	Those Bandanas are neighborhood boys.
ASHLEY:	They're thugs!
BERNICE:	Now, now, Ashley. Remember they are God's children, too.
ASHLEY:	But there are so many thugs, you can't even go out alone in that neighborhood.
BERNICE:	Honey, I can't even get down the stairs by myself. That's why the YMCA bus driver comes up to help me down the stairs and to the grocery store.
ASHLEY:	Aren't you afraid?
BERNICE:	I have two secret weapons.
ASHLEY:	Good! You have a gun.
BERNICE:	Nah! Don't need one. I have God. When I'm afraid, I talk to him. Then I feel better.
ASHLEY:	What's the other weapon?
BERNICE:	*(Laughs)* My right arm is insured by Lloyds of London as a lethal weapon.

ASHLEY:	You're kidding?
BERNICE:	And on the outside chance a thief might get into my apartment, I have The Bucket!
ASHLEY:	What bucket?
BERNICE:	If a thief steals from me, I can identify him. The bucket is full of red dye. Everything he carries and everything he wears will be, excuse the pun, hot pink.
ASHLEY:	*(Laughs and laughs)* Bernice-with-the-bucket, you bowl me over.
BERNICE:	A person can't be too careful. I'm careful, that's all.
ASHLEY:	I've wasted all that worry about you for the half hour when you didn't answer the phone. I thought you'd been mugged by the Bandanas.
BERNICE:	I don't answer the phone when I'm in prayer.
ASHLEY:	Do you pray every morning?
BERNICE:	I usually begin my day with prayer. Today I was praying for the Bandanas.
ASHLEY:	No! How can that help?
BERNICE:	Prayer gives me a new way of looking at them.
ASHLEY:	They're dangerous any way you look at them.
BERNICE:	Just the same they might be influenced.
ASHLEY:	By you or God?
BERNICE:	Who knows? We may not know how God uses our prayer, but he does.
ASHLEY:	I call to cheer you up, and you give me a bunch of things to think about.
BERNICE:	But you *did* cheer me. Tell me what you're doing today.
ASHLEY:	This is my half day to work. How about you?
BERNICE:	A little television. And with cold weather coming, I plan to start a black sweater for Binnie.
ASHLEY:	Binnie who?
BERNICE:	I don't know his name. He's the tallest Bandana—the one with the loud, black bike.

DRAMA 3: THE ALBUM
Why intercessory prayer?

Production Notes

Characters: Dad, Paul (seven to fifteen years old), Moderator.
Playing time: 3 minutes

Properties: A picture album with three loose picture post cards, a coffee mug, newspaper, and a soft drink can.

Costumes: Casual clothes appropriate for all ages.

Setting: A corner of a living room. One easy chair for Dad, a large cushion for Paul, and a stack of books or bookshelves with books.

MODERATOR:	If you have ever wondered why you should pray for someone, you will want to listen closely to the After Dinner Players for some clues to intercessory prayer.
	(PAUL is seated on a cushion in the midst of books or next to the bookcase looking at a large photograph album. Next to him is a canned soft drink. DAD is seated nearby drinking coffee and reading the newspaper.)
DAD:	*(Lowering paper)* You've been looking at that picture a long time.
PAUL:	I was thinking about God.
DAD:	*(Chuckles)* Do we have a picture of him in there?
PAUL:	Aw, com'on, Dad. Be serious.
DAD:	Okay. I'm serious. *(Folds newspaper and places in his lap)* What were you thinking?
PAUL:	It's the post card Aunt Catherine sent us. *(Holds up card)*
DAD:	*(Reaches for card)* Which one?
PAUL:	The seashore scene. *(Hands it to DAD)* I can almost hear the sea gulls and the waves rolling over and over.
DAD:	It is beautiful.
PAUL:	Looking at it made me feel the same way I did last summer on vacation.
DAD:	In the mountains?
PAUL:	Yeah. I felt close to God. The sky and trees and the blue lake were so beautiful, I just had to say thank you to God for his creation.
DAD:	Good thing to do.
PAUL:	*(Looking in album)* And here's another picture Aunt Catherine sent from Switzerland. Look at the snow! *(Hands the card to DAD)*
DAD:	Magnificent! And so real looking I feel cold.
PAUL:	*(Turns another card from the album over and picks up to read message)* Why does Aunt Catherine always sign her name "with love and prayers"?
DAD:	She once told me that she prays for you every day.
PAUL:	Why?

DAD:	It's one way of showing her love.
PAUL:	I mean, why does she pray for me?
DAD:	Maybe it helps her understand you better. Or maybe it's her way of honoring you. Maybe she believes God will give you special help. Why don't you write and ask her why she prays for you?
PAUL:	I'd feel stupid doing that.
DAD:	It's a smart question, and I'll bet she'd like to answer.
PAUL:	I have a great idea. Let's go to Switzerland.
DAD:	If you start saving money now, you could go by the year 2020.
PAUL:	I'll be an old man!
DAD:	So what's so bad about that?
PAUL:	I'd rather go now.
DAD:	I think you have the right idea when you think about God wherever you are or however you feel. Until you save all that money just think about him close to home.
PAUL:	*(Picks another photograph)* Hey, here's a picture of you in your plant uniform and hard hat.
DAD:	Now there's something you could thank God for.
PAUL:	What?
DAD:	The big layoff didn't get me.
PAUL:	What if it does next month?
DAD:	With God's help we will manage.

Moderator leads in applause and sends persons into groups. Provide assistance for those who need help in moving chairs.

SMALL GROUPS

Discussion questions for a retreat may be found on pp. 72-73.

The dramas have slightly different themes. In the first, Barbara told us about her place of prayer and what she prayed for. In the second, Bernice told us that prayer was to be in the world for the world, and it required her to do something. In the third, Paul wondered why Aunt Catherine prayed for him.

1. What questions do you have about any of these ideas?
2. Where do you like to pray?

3. What happens when you pray? (A broad question designed to adjust to your group.)
4. In many ways, prayer is a mystery. We may never fully understand why or how prayer works, but it does. How has prayer helped you?
5. Jesus said a lot about prayer. He also taught his disciples a prayer that we call the Lord's Prayer. Read it from Matthew 6:9-13.

CLOSING

Close your group meeting with sentence prayers or recite the Lord's Prayer as we know it today. Pass out the pretzel recipe and the pretzels. Follow with drinks. The pretzels are salty!

ALTERNATE ACTIVITIES

To make a family blessing tri-fold, reproduce the following prayers (or ones you have written), cut them out, glue on cardboard or construction paper so that a prayer is visible from each of the two top sides of the fold. The prayer standard rests on the third fold. Decorate if you like.

Because we are yours, we live in gratitude for your blessings. Thank you for the love we share at our table. Help us to be kind and loving. Amen.

Dear God, Thank you for the beautiful world you created and for the beautiful people who live in it. Help us to take care of the world. Help us notice the needs of other persons. Thank you for food to eat. Teach us to share. Amen.

To adapt the dramas for separate use at a retreat, use the following questions, which are geared toward older children, youth, and adults:

DRAMA 1: SINGING IN THE SHOWER

1. Barbara believed that regular prayer would be helpful, so she used a regular activity as a reminder to pray. To what other activities could she have tied her prayer?
2. Where and when do you or someone you know pray? (This makes a good charade question. Have persons pantomime for each other the times and/or places they pray.)
3. Where or when do (or did) your parents pray?
4. What do you expect when you pray? Have you ever used God as a Santa Claus to try to get what you want?
5. The scripture tells us about some of the times Jesus withdrew to pray. Read Matthew 26:36; Luke 23:32-34; Mark 1:35, 6:30-32, 6:46; and Luke 5:15. What clues about prayer life did you get from these scriptures? Keep in mind that we have only a few records of Jesus' personal habits, but we can guess that Jesus lived in a spirit of joy and gratitude to God.
6. What prayer goals would you like to set for yourself in the next

twenty-four hours? Or what would you like to try before our next session? Would you like to pray with someone from our group?

DRAMA 2: BERNICE TALKS

1. In the dialogue between Bernice and Ashley, you noticed that Bernice usually begins her day with prayer. Is that a good time for you? Please comment or ask questions about your prayer experimentation since the last session.
2. What happened when Bernice prayed? (She said it gave her a new way of looking at things, but she also said she doesn't know how God uses prayer.)
3. What action did Bernice take on her prayers?
4. What action did you take on your prayers since our last meeting? Must you always take action?
5. During the few minutes of silence we will observe now, review what you have prayed for in the last week. (Silence.) Were you asking God to play Santa Claus? To help you? Guide you? Heal you? Was there thankfulness in your prayers?
6. To live in Christ is to grow in Christ. Do you think Bernice has changed her prayer life over the years?
7. The questions of the group are extremely important. If you run out of time, write the questions and begin there at the third session.

DRAMA 3: THE ALBUM

1. What happened as a result of Aunt Catherine's prayers for Paul? Do we know?
2. When we pray for someone besides ourselves, can we be sure our prayer is answered?
3. Read scripture on prayer: Luke 6:27-28; Philippians 4:6; I Thessalonians 5:16-18, 25-28; James 5:16; Psalm 86:6-7; and Matthew 6:9-13. Summarize what each scripture snatch says to you about prayer.

EVENT THEME:
THINKING TIME WITH GOD

SCHEDULE

*Get nametags and browse display tables.
*Focus Activity:
   1. At tables, make "Thinking Time with God" booklets.
   2. Perform skit, "Get Out of the Apple Tree or You'll Break Your Arm" or
   3. the monologue, "Simeon Sits Toward Heaven" (for older groups).
*Sharing Time:
   1. If it is a small group, share feelings and ideas about thinking with God.
   2. If it is a large group, close with the song "This Is My Father's World," and read a prayer from "Thinking Time with God" booklet.

ADVANCE PREPARATION

*Recruit a moderator.
*Recruit one chairperson for each ten to twelve persons for making booklets.
*Collect supplies for making booklets. See sample at the end of the monologue.
*Ask the congregation to bring personal devotional books for a display. Include Bibles and Bible story books.
*Recruit a person to receive books brought for the display table.
*Select a drama director who will recruit actors and rehearse skit or monologue. (See introduction, p. 5.)
*Recruit a song leader to teach and lead songs.
*Recruit a refreshment committee.

ROOM ARRANGEMENT

*Chairs for ten to twelve persons around each table. Bookmaking supplies should be on each table.
*Display tables for devotional books.

THINKING TIME WITH GOD

This booklet belongs to

MY WORLD

How wonderful that God created the universe! It is wonderfully crafted with dependable laws and beauty. An appreciation of the stars and space and creatures in the woods and on the beaches makes life richer. Knowing that God created humankind makes life more important. "Everything God created is good" (I Timothy 4:4a) and we are God's hands, minds, and energy to keep it that way.

THINKING TIME:

I will think of ways I can help keep God's world clean, unpolluted, and sparkling fresh. I can't do everything at once, but I can do something TODAY. And I can plan for the future. I will ask myself, "What can I do for God's world that will benefit it today, next week, and in the years to come?" I will think with God about it. I will do what is necessary to educate myself about his world and my job as a caretaker.

MY PRAYER

Prayer is important for everyone. Even Jesus prayed! After leaving a crowd that was gathered by the lake, "He went up on a mountainside to pray" (Mark 6:46). Another time he got up from sleeping while it was still dark, left the house, and went off to be alone where he prayed (Mark 1:35). for those who believe in God and feel that his energy is present in us and in the everyday world, talking to God is very important.

THINKING TIME:

Because prayer will help my relationship with God and persons around me, I will talk to God and think with him. I will listen for his nudges and urgings. I will think about what He might want me to do. The Bible tells me not to worry about anything, "but in everything, by prayer and petition, with thanksgiving, present your requests to God" (Philippians 4:6). I will try this and keep on trying until I learn what it really means. God will help me.

MY JOY AND THANKSGIVING

Shout for joy to the Lord, all the earth.
Worship the Lord with gladness;
   come before him with joyful songs (Psalm 100:1-2).
Sing to him the songs you know. Clap your hands and make music in your heart. Recite his wonderful acts.
Glory in his holy name; let the hearts of those who seek the Lord rejoice. Look to the Lord and his strength; seek his face always (Psalm 105:2-4 paraphrase).

THINKING TIME:

As I sit quietly, thinking with God, I name the persons and things for which I am thankful. I remember that God loves me and blesses me. I will sing songs I know about God, especially songs of thanks and love. I will find a way or ways to express the joy that wells up inside me when I think of the blessings in my life. I will think harder if I think I have no blessings. Then I will say, "Yeah, Yeah, God!"

MY SHARING AND CARING

Jesus told his disciples that when they fed the hungry or gave a drink to a thirsty person they honored him the same as if they did those things for him. He went on to mention other sharing and compassionate deeds that honored him such as making a stranger welcome, taking care of sick persons, clothing the needy, and visiting persons in many kinds of prisons (Matthew 25:35-40). Other New Testament scriptures remind us to share with God's people who are in need and to practice hospitality (Romans 12:13).

THINKING TIME:

I think now about how I can share my time and properties with someone less fortunate. For TODAY I will think of a way to share. Persons or groups I know may have projects I can join later.

MY WATCHDOG

You are the watchdog of your own life because you can make Christian decisions about what you want to do. Even when events challenge your behavior or health, you can decide how you will meet these events. Your attitude can be the same as that of Jesus (Philippians 2:5). Think about what is true, noble, pure, right, lovely, and excellent. Think about whatever is admirable and worthy of praise (Philippians 4:8).

THINKING TIME:

I am reminded to concentrate on good and healthy living and thinking. In doing this I do not need to seek out friends or entertainment that is bad for me. I can avoid participating in activities that are not healthy and wholesome for my life as a Christian. I think now about choices I can make at school and in my recreation that are admirable and worthy of me as a child of God.

MY PEACEMAKING

Peace is always more desirable than war or trouble and tension between persons or groups. Finding a peaceful solution to a problem requires thought. Then it usually requires action. Sometimes saying, "I'm sorry," is enough. Often discussion or listening to the other person's point of view helps. Some problems are so big they require the use of a mediator (third person) or counselor. Victims of violence or abuse discover that talking about the violence or abuse with a trusted adult friend helps.

THINKING TIME:

As I sit quietly, I remember an argument or a problem about which I am angry or concerned. I will consider ways the problem might be settled without violence or bad feelings. Considering what I know about Jesus, I will try to copy his attitude toward people and disagreements.

Let the peace of Christ rule in your hearts, since as members of one body you were called to peace (Colossians 3:15).

MY PATH IN LIFE

The psalmist makes the same request of God that many Christians make today: "Show me your ways, O Lord; *teach me your paths.* Guide me in your truth, and teach me, for you are God my Savior . . ." (Psalm 25:4-5) One of Jesus' disciples, Peter, wrote his friends to tell them how to walk a Christian pathway. He said, "Follow in his [Jesus'] steps" (1 Peter 2:21).

THINKING TIME:

As I take time out to thank God today, I will give thanks that God walks with me every day along the path of life, helping me stay on the Christian pathway.

And I will think about Jesus and how I can follow his steps. I will recall how he loved and served other persons and how he lived a life in which persons were more important than things. How can I use his teachings in my life? Do I need to know more about Jesus? I will think about how to learn more.

*Put chairs in front of staging area or have participants move them. Aid persons with handicapping conditions.
*Play the piano or autoharp for closing song.

AS PEOPLE ARRIVE

*Make nametags.
*Take devotional books to central display table. Check for names and phone numbers in front of the books.
*The moderator directs persons to activity tables.

FOCUS ACTIVITY

1. Chairpersons explain to groups what they will be making and how to make it.

    Directions and pattern for making "Thinking Time with God" booklet:

    1. Reproduce the pattern, printing front and back.
    2. Cut on dashed line.
    3. Fold on dotted line to form booklet.
    4. Cut eight-and-a-half-by-eleven-inch colored construction paper in half lengthwise. Fold one piece over the formed booklet.
    5. Open the booklet to the centerfold. Staple with two staples. Fold shut.
    6. Decorate cover. Write your name on the back.

2. Skit

GET OUT OF THE APPLE TREE
OR YOU'LL BREAK YOUR ARM

Production Notes

Characters: Mother, Dad, Cliff (seventeen years old), Grandmother, Carol (nine to ten years old), event moderator.

Playing time: 8-10 minutes.

Properties: "Thinking Time with God" booklet, a pan filled with vegetables, water in a pitcher, glasses, a table and setting for five persons, chairs, a telephone on a long table, a sack with bottle of pills, and an armful of books.

Setting: The Lockett family kitchen just before supper. A table is downstage with five chairs arranged so no one sits with his or her back to the audience. Another table representing kitchen cabinets holds a telephone, some books, a copy of "Thinking Time with God," a pitcher of water and glasses, a pan of vegetables, and a bowl. The scene requires a door, real or imaginary. Except for the table, chairs, and booklet, properties may be imaginary if characters exaggerate their actions.

MODERATOR:	The Thinking Time Players present a playlet, "Get Out of the Apple Tree or You'll Break Your Arm." The scene opens as Mom and Dad Lockett set the table for supper. *(Sits in audience)*
DAD:	*(Placing silver on table)* So he told me to fake the report or find another job!
MOM:	*(Setting plates on table)* No! What did you say to that?
DAD:	I said I'd think about it.
MOM:	*(Stops action)* That will take a lot of thinking!
DAD:	But I keep thinking in circles.
	(Enter CLIFF followed by GRANDMOTHER)
CLIFF:	*(Dropping books to floor away from table)* Problems, problems everywhere!
GRANDMOTHER:	*(Placing sack from drugstore on table and taking out bottle of pills)* And more problems!
MOM:	Here, too.
DAD:	What's yours?
GRANDMOTHER:	Just the usual arthritis.
DAD:	*(To CLIFF)* What's yours?
CLIFF:	Mr. White accused me of cheating on the math test.
MOM:	That's crazy!
GRANDMOTHER:	Not you!
DAD:	Did you?
CLIFF:	Course not!
MOM:	Then why did he accuse you?
CLIFF:	I think Harry copied off my paper.
GRANDMOTHER:	Your best friend copied? *(Sits at the table)*
DAD:	You sure?
CLIFF:	No, but our seats are next to each other, and Harry missed the same problem.
MOM:	You missed only one? *(Stirs vegetables in pan)*

DAD:	*(To* MOM) Don't sound so surprised. He studied half the night for that test. And I quizzed him.
CLIFF:	I know the material and I didn't cheat.
MOM:	*(Stops stirring, turns to* CLIFF) Just tell Mr. White.
CLIFF:	There's more. Mr. White tore my paper into shreds in front of the class and *(Pause)*
DAD:	And what?
CLIFF:	After class Donna said she didn't want to be seen with a cheater, ever.
DAD:	Oh, man! This one's going to take some thought.
MOM:	And it will take a long time. Let's talk about it after supper. Someone call Carol.
DAD:	*(Calls out the door)* Carol! Hey, Carol! Supper's ready.
MOM:	*(To* CLIFF) Will you put the water on the table?
	(CLIFF *pours the water and* DAD *puts vegetables in the bowl and puts it on the table while* MOM *looks out the door.)*
MOM:	Carol! Get out of the apple tree! You'll break your arm.
	(Silence)
MOM:	I said stop sitting in that tree.
DAD:	*(Goes to door)* Come on. Supper's ready.
MOM:	*(Going to the table)* We've got to do something about her. Every day she sits in the top of the apple tree.
CLIFF:	I sat there for years.
MOM:	Yes, but you were older.
	(CAROL *enters)*
CAROL:	You ruined my thinking!
MOM:	You think about washing your hands.
	(While CAROL *washes her hands at an imaginary sink, the others sit at the table.* CAROL *joins them, then jumps up and runs to the table near the telephone where she gets her "Thinking Time with God" booklet.)*
CLIFF:	Come on, Carol.
CAROL:	But we haven't had our table prayer.
CLIFF:	I'm in a hurry.
DAD:	*(Humoring her)* All right, get on with it.

CAROL: *(Opens booklet and reads haltingly)* Thank you, God, for our home and for this food. *(Looks at family)* Aw, com'on. Bow your heads. It's a sign of rev . . . reverence.

(They bow their heads.)

CAROL: Most of all, God, thank you for the love in our family. Amen.

(Family members shift in their seats and act surprised and a little embarrassed.)

MOM: That was a nice prayer.

DAD: Where did you get that little book?

CAROL: I made it at Sunday school. See, it says, "Thinking Time with God." *(Holds book up)*

MOM: We have a lot to think about tonight. Everyone has problems.

DAD: You have a problem, Carol. Please stay out of the apple tree before you fall.

CAROL: My Sunday school teacher told us we should go someplace special to think about God. So I sit in the tree.

CLIFF: I used to sit up there to spy on Charley Harelson.

MOM: But you were twelve years old.

CAROL: But it's quiet up there. No one bothers me.

DAD: We all think in the kitchen and in the car. They're safe places.

CAROL: Mrs. Harelson says there's a difference between just thinking and taking time out to think with God and think about God.

CLIFF: Who did you say?

CAROL: God.

CLIFF: No, the first name.

CAROL: Mrs. Harelson.

CLIFF: Charley's mother?

CAROL: How would I know? She's just my Sunday school teacher. I like her.

MOM: Did she say how you should think with God?

CAROL: She said everyone has a different way. We made this little book of Bible verses and prayers to help us think. Tonight I'm thinking about what Jesus would do if someone stole his sandwich in the lunch room.

CLIFF:	That thinking sounds like a Vulcan mind weld from "Star Trek."
GRANDMOTHER:	It's more complicated than that.
MOM:	Carol, you have given us some good ideas for our own problems. Maybe we could borrow your thinking book.
CAROL:	You're big. You could use the Bible.
DAD:	*(Laughing)* We should have known that.
GRANDMOTHER:	What about kids who can't read or people who can't see?
CAROL:	I guess they could think about the "Jesus Loves Me" song or just talk to God. Mrs. Harelson said you just do what you can. No problem.
MOM:	But Carol, you still have a problem.
CAROL:	What?
MOM:	Stay out of the apple tree until the apples get ripe. We'll use a ladder to pick the apples. You find a safe place for thinking with God.
CAROL:	I tried behind the dresser, but someone kept pushing the dresser back.
MOM:	Me.
CAROL:	I tried the back seat of the car, but someone kept locking it.
DAD:	Me.
CLIFF:	Try your room with the door shut.
MOM:	We'll stay out.
CAROL:	*(With surprise and indignation)* My room! That's so . . . so . . . ordinary.

The moderator should lead applause for the actors.

If the group is small, discuss the play and/or use the following questions. If the group is large, consider using the questions in small groups when the "Thinking Time" booklets are made.

QUESTIONS

1. Do you know anyone who takes time out often to think with God, pray, or read the Bible? When does he or she do it?
2. Many times parents read their Bibles in private. Have you ever seen your parents read the Bible? What message did it give you? (This question is for everyone.)

3. To meditate is to open the mind so completely to a thought (for example, honesty, God, justice, Jesus) that there is no place for anything else. If you have a special place or time for thinking with God (some people call it meditating), please tell us where and when it is. What problems have you encountered in doing this?

CLOSING TIME

Sing songs familiar to your children such as "Jesus Loves Me." Post a copy of the words to "This Is My Father's World" (see p. 84). Say words line by line after playing the song. Sing the song more than once.

SIMEON SITS TOWARD HEAVEN
Monologue

Production Notes

Characters: Blefir, event moderator.
Playing time: 2 minutes.
Properties: Basket or bucket, and a long rope.
Costume: Tunic and sandals or cloak and robe.
Arrange seats in a circle around the staging area.

MODERATOR: Early monks, and later hermits, felt that living in the world hindered their constant prayer and Bible reading. Many of them went into caves to be alone. During that time, they would pray, meditate, and read the Bible. They also went without food and sleep as a sign to God that they were seriously dedicated to him. One of these hermits was Simeon Stylites, who spent the last part of his life on top of a pillar in Syria. Of course, Simeon needed the help of a ground crew. We hear from one of them, Blefir, in this drama. *(Sits in audience)*

BLEFIR: (BLEFIR *enters carrying a bucket or basket and a coil of long rope. Stands stage left looking up thirty feet stage right.)*

Simeon! Oh, Simeon! *(Pause)* Answer me. I know you're up there.

(Pause) Okay. Don't talk.

(Ties rope to the handle of the basket as he talks.)

Do you know how hard it is to talk to someone who's thirty feet up? Come on down.

(Pause)

Forty days is long enough to talk to God. Don't you think he wants to hear from someone else? *(Pause)* Besides, you're giving me a pain in my neck.

(Lies down on back to look upward)

Listen, Simeon, Jesus has been dead two hundred years. But if he walked past here today, instead of saying, "Take up your bed and walk," he would say "Come down off that pillar and take care of yourself."

(Listens intently)

No, I haven't seen him lately. But I've read the Good Book myself.

(Rises from ground, prepares bucket, then looks upward)

I know you're thinking about God—nothing wrong with that—it's just that *(Lowers head and rubs neck, speaking to the ground)*, God forgive me for complaining. *(Shouts)* We have a whole special duty set up just to bring you food. *(Kicks the bucket)*

(Listens)

No, it's not good food, just food. And brother Amura is taking your garden duty, and I'm taking your kitchen duty. We're getting tired. Why do you continue doing this? No one said you didn't know how to pray. You don't have to prove anything.

(Listens a long time)

You say God likes it this way?

(Walks around and around the pillar then picks up the bucket and throws the rope into the air)

Who am I to argue with God?

DISCUSSION QUESTIONS

1. If you had to vote, would your sympathies lie with Simeon Stylites or his long-suffering friend, Blefir?
2. What is the longest amount of time you have known anyone to meditate? Who was it?
3. Why don't more persons take time out to pray, read the Bible, or think with God?
4. Do you know someone whose life has been enriched by a special spiritual time?
5. What is the difference between taking time with God by intent and having good intentions?

If response has been focused and serious, the moderator might ask if the group is interested in undertaking serious daily time out with God. The benefits of such a time are not always quickly evident. The group might want to meet again to share feelings and discuss doubts, problems, or joys.

This Is My Father's World

Maltbie D. Babcock

TERRA BEATA
Trad. English melody
adapt. by Franklin L. Sheppard

1. This is my Father's world, and to my lis-tening ears all na-ture sings, and round me rings the mu-sic of the spheres. This is my Fa-ther's world: I rest me in the thought of rocks and trees, of skies and seas; his hand the won-ders wrought.

2. This is my Father's world, the birds their car-ols raise, the morn-ing light, the lil-y white, de-clare their mak-er's praise. This is my Fa-ther's world: he shines in all that's fair; in the rust-ling grass I hear him pass; he speaks to me ev-ery-where.

3. This is my Father's world, O let me ne'er for-get that tho the wrong seems oft so strong, God is the rul-er yet. This is my Fa-ther's world: why should my heart be sad? The Lord is King; let the heav-ens ring! God reigns; let the earth be glad!

EVENT THEME:
THE MEANING OF THE CHURCH

SCHEDULE

*Get nametags.
*Get Together Activity:
   1. Browse through a display of pictures.
   2. Or as an alternate activity, leave food for the needy.
*Have refreshments or a meal.
*Focus Activity:
   1. Puppet show: "The Detective Agency."
   2. Announce winners of the picture contest.
*Sharing Time:
   1. Games.
   2. Goodnight circle.

ADVANCE PREPARATION

*Publicize a picture of the church contest. Request that pictures illustrate the church in action, the church building, and church friends. Recruit chairperson for displaying and judging pictures by age groups divided into children, youth, and adults.
*Plan refreshment or a meal.
*Recruit a puppet show director, properties manager, and stage manager. (See introduction p. 5.) The puppet show can be produced by any youth group.
*Recruit a game leader.
*Buy or make best picture awards.

ROOM ARRANGEMENT

*Have a nametag table.
*Hang pictures of the church in the hallway or around the walls of your meeting room.
*Arrange for a puppet stage, or make one from a refrigerator shipping box. Place the stage between two tables turned on their edges where readers may

be hidden. Puppet stage must be in front of a wall on which pictures of scenery may be hung.

*Children sit on the floor in front of the stage. Arrange chairs for others behind the sitting area.

AS PEOPLE ARRIVE

*Get nametags and hang pictures in designated areas.
*Browse through pictures.

FOCUS ACTIVITY

THE DETECTIVE AGENCY
A puppet play about the meaning of the church.

The church mouse consults the Bow Wow Detective Agency to discover what the church really is.

This puppet show may also be acted out on a stage as a playlet, or videotaped. Any presentation needs a director, properties coordinator, and stage manager. This puppet play is easy to perform. It was written and performed for children by an eighth-grade Sunday school class at Chapelwood United Methodist Church in Houston, Texas.

Production Notes

Characters: Scratch, an absent-minded dog detective who repeats himself a lot and carries a large magnifying glass; Bones, a dog detective who often peers over, around, and under things for clues; Cindy, the church mouse; Mission Man; Minister; Sam, a little boy; and Julie, a little girl. Puppeteers do actions; voices are provided by seven readers who sit on the floor next to the puppet stage concealed from the audience by a table turned on its edge.

Playing time: 10-12 minutes, plus singing time between scenes.

Properties: Magnifying glass, eye glasses, tape player, and tape of children singing "We Are the Church" (*The United Methodist Hymnal,* hymn 558).

Settings: Backdrops are drawn on bulletin board paper, placed in view behind the stage and layered so that the last scene is on bottom, and scene one is on top. At the end of each scene, remove the top sheet, revealing the setting for the next scene.

Scene I: A detective office containing a desk, stage left, and a sign, stage right, announcing the name "Bow Wow Detective Agency."

Scene II: A large hallway showing only the area at floor level—a large mouse hole in the baseboard, the bottoms of doors, and large feet that seem about to walk on the three characters in the scene.

Scene III: The church office with a desk and back of chair. One portion of the wall might contain framed drawings of the minister, secretary, choir director, and janitor. A money box is on its side and money spilled on the desk.

Scene IV: Church sanctuary, looking toward the altar.

Scene V: A swing set or slide on the school playground. Draw a few children around the slide.

SCENE I

(SCRATCH *is in front of the desk, stage left, in the detective agency.* BONES *is standing stage right. A knock is heard and* SCRATCH *moves and calls to stage left.*)

SCRATCH: Come in! Come in! *(Moves to desk)*

(CINDY *enters from left and passes to stand by* BONES.)

CINDY: Thanks. I'm glad you can see me today.

BONES: We are always glad to make room on our schedule for someone who needs a mystery solved.

SCRATCH: *(Scratching head)* What is your problem?

CINDY: It's a little hard to describe, being who I am.

BONES: Well, who are you?

CINDY: I'm Cindy Mouse. I'm a church mouse.

SCRATCH: That doesn't sound very mysterious.

CINDY: Hold on. I'll explain. I have lived all my life in a nice church. It has a cool fountain where I take my shower, and a neat kitchen where I crumb my meals.

BONES: Sounds like a great place to live. What's the mystery?

CINDY: My bedroom is in the wall between the first and second grade Sunday school classes. Every Sunday I peep out of my holes and watch the children. Recently they have been studying about the church. The mystery is this: They keep saying the church is not a building. How can that be?

BONES: The church is not a building? But you live there. It is a building.

SCRATCH: Yet the children and teachers must be right. What clues do you have that might help us find out what the church really is?

CINDY: Silly! If I had clues and could solve this mystery, would I be consulting two detectives? *You're* supposed to help *me!*

BONES: Okay. Okay. Don't get your ears up about it. We'll help you solve the mystery.

SCRATCH: The first thing we must do is meet you at the scene of the mystery where we can look and listen for clues.

CINDY: Okay. Meet me Sunday morning at 9:45 A.M. in the front hall next to the playground.

(Characters exit stage left. Prop Manager removes backdrop from stage right. Setting for scene two is revealed.)

SCENE II

(SCRATCH, BONES, and CINDY enter stage left. They appear to be lost in a sea of feet in the hallway.)

CINDY: Right this way to the second-grade classroom.

BONES: *(Dodging feet)* That pair of tennis shoes almost got me!

SCRATCH: These folks surely have big feet. Watch it!

("We Are the Church" plays softly.)

CINDY: Do you hear it?

BONES: Hear what?

SCRATCH: I hear some birds.

(The music gets louder.)

CINDY: *(Impatiently)* No, listen.

BONES: Better keep moving, or get walked on.

SCRATCH: I hear music. I hear music.

BONES: What kind of music?

SCRATCH: *(Holding up magnifying glass)* I'll see. I'll see.

BONES: Think! You have to listen to music. You can't see it!

SCRATCH: *(Putting down magnifying glass)* So you do. So you do.

(They all listen to "We Are the Church.")

BONES: *(Shouting)* Clue! Clue!

SCRATCH: What clue? What clue?

CINDY: People.

BONES: The church is people. Madame, your mystery is solved. The song says the church is people.

CINDY: But the church has to be more than that. The song says so.

SCRATCH: So it does. So it does.

BONES: Okay. Let's look for more clues. Walk this way—be careful of those feet.

(Actors leave stage left as Prop Manager removes the backdrop, stage right, revealing the setting for scene three.)

SCENE III

(CINDY, BONES, and SCRATCH are peering out from behind a chair or over the top of a desk in the church office. A box of money is spilled on the desk.)

CINDY: I avoid this place. There is too much noise here.

SCRATCH: This looks like a great place for clues. A great place for clues.

CINDY: How can it look like a clue place?

BONES: There are lots of desks that could have many fingerprints. And there are lots of telephones that could have mysterious calls.

CINDY: Well, when I've been here, the phone calls have all been about helping someone who is sick or has a new baby. They talk a lot about names and addresses.

BONES: Then there is no mystery about this place. It is probably just the headquarters for the whole operation.

CINDY: But what do they do with all that money? *(The trio moves toward the spilled money)*

SCRATCH: Let's find out. Let's find out.

BONES: Quick! Hide! Someone is coming.

(Enter MISSION MAN and MINISTER, stage right.)

MISSION MAN: Look! The money has been spilled. I hope none of it was lost or stolen. Our missions program needs every cent it can get.

MINISTER: Don't worry; our treasurer keeps track of every penny. And more and more people make donations. That is one of the great things about the Christian church—people share with the needy.

(At this point in the script you may elect to show slides of your church's outreach program. Project them on the front of the puppet stage on which you have placed a white posterboard. If slides are not available, have your youth group research the mission outreach of your local church and make slides. Another option is to incorporate a few facts about church outreach into the script between MINISTER and MISSION MAN. Afterwards, MISSION MAN and MINISTER exit.)

CINDY: Is donating the same as stealing?

BONES: Not at all. When people choose to give money, it's called a donation. People give so that the church can have money to send to places where it is needed. Some people are in need because they are sick. Others are hungry. Even others want to build a church or buy Bibles.

CINDY: So they collect money to send to places like that?

BONES: This is really a good clue. It might help answer our question, "What is the church?"

SCRATCH: The church helps in all kinds of ways. It might even help you.

CINDY: How could it help me? I thought I was supposed to help it.

BONES: When you donate money to the church, some of it stays right in the church to help with the recreation center, buy paper, buy Sunday school books, and even to build new rooms.

CINDY: Oh, so that's how they use all that money they collect. I see it in big round plates sometimes after church. Is that different money from what we see in the box?

SCRATCH: The box says missions. This must be a special project.

CINDY: If I were not such an honest mouse I might want to take some of this green money back into the wall and pad my bed with it. Folded money would be really soft.

BONES: Watch it! Remember that you are a church mouse. Thou shalt not steal.

                  (Actors exit stage left. Prop Manager, stage right, removes backdrop revealing setting for next scene.)

SCENE IV

                  (CINDY, SCRATCH, and BONES are next to a large seat in the sanctuary. They look down the aisle toward the sanctuary, then face the audience as they talk. Organ music is playing very softly in the background.)

SCRATCH: This is so big!

BONES: And it's pretty and nice. I haven't been in a church sanctuary for a long, long time.

CINDY: I come here all the time, but mostly when people are not here. For some reason, they seem to get scared and jump around when I come in.

SCRATCH: Well, for goodness sake, stay out of sight.

BONES: Stay back. Stay back.

CINDY: Okay. They probably wouldn't be too pleased about having a couple of dogs hanging around here either.

SCRATCH: Where is that music coming from?

BONES: Pretty music.

CINDY: That's the chancel choir. That man in front of them is Mr. Evans. See! He's waving his arms around. That's how he directs the choir.

SCRATCH: Who's in the choir?

BONES: That's a dumb question. Even I know the answer. Anyone can be in the choir.

SCRATCH: But what if you can't sing? I howl.

CINDY: They have choir practice all the time. They teach you to sing.

SCRATCH: Shhh. That man is standing up to talk. Be careful, or they will see and hear us.

CINDY: That's Dr. Williams. He's the senior minister at this church. He's preaching.

BONES: Preaching? What's that?

CINDY: He explains things about being a Christian. He reads from the Bible.

SCRATCH: What else do you hear in the sanctuary? What else?

CINDY: I have heard them say prayers together, and sometimes they do something called communion. At Christmas they decorate a huge tree and bring presents.

BONES: Sounds busy.

CINDY: The church is busy—busy people worshiping and working together.

BONES: That's a clue. Write it down. It's important.

              (Actors exit stage left. Prop Manager, stage right, removes scenery and sets stage for last scene.)

SCENE V

(CINDY, SCRATCH, *and* BONES *enter stage left and stand next to a playground slide.* SAM *enters stage right and stands at edge of the stage.)*

BONES:	Look, there's a little boy crying. He must be lost.
SCRATCH:	He needs help—really needs help.
CINDY:	Look! Someone's coming. Maybe she will help him.
SCRATCH:	Not likely. Not likely.

(Enter JULIE *stage right. She walks to the boy.)*

JULIE:	Are you lost?
SCRATCH:	*(Long silence)*
JULIE:	Are you scared?
SAM:	*(Long silence)*
JULIE:	I've been scared before. I know what it feels like. Are you looking for your mother?
SAM:	*(Nods yes)*
JULIE:	I think I saw her back by the water fountain. She's looking for you. Come on. Take my hand, and we'll walk together to your mother.

(They walk off right.)

CINDY:	Was that girl one we saw at the church yesterday?
BONES:	She looked familiar.
SCRATCH:	She was kind to the lost boy.
BONES:	She seemed in a hurry to go someplace, so she really went out of her way to help.
CINDY:	Does her kindness have something to do with where we saw her—at the church?
SCRATCH:	By George! I think I've got it. I've got it.
BONES:	Got what?
SCRATCH:	The answer: the church is not just a building—it is people. It's people helping people wherever they are; they don't have to be at church.
CINDY:	Julie was part of the church at church, yet she is the church on the playground. Even I can be the church mouse when I'm at the cheese market or school yard. Wherever I am, I'm the church. What a great idea!
BONES:	Your case is solved. The Bow Wow Detective Agency rests its case. That will be $200.
CINDY:	What if I pay the detective agency half of that and give the rest to the missions box?

SCRATCH: Great idea! Great idea!

BONES: It is?

Curtain

DISCUSSION QUESTIONS

Suitable for older children, youth, and adults:
1. There is a visible church—the building, services, and people in it. The not-so-noticeable church takes a different form. According to the puppet show, where did the characters find the not-so-noticeable church?
2. Where do you see the not-so-noticeable church in your community?
3. If you do not see that influence in your community, how can you change the image?
4. How are you involved in both types of church?

GAMES

Church Sculpture

Divide into groups of ten to twenty people.

Explain that the church has voted to build a statue in front of the church to portray teamwork (or outreach, or harmony, or joy). Each group selects five persons to be the lumps of clay. Give groups from three to five minutes to create a statue portraying your selected theme. Share statues. Continue with more statues.*

Long Johns and Balloons

Supplies: Balloons and extra large long johns.

Divide into groups of ten to fifteen people. Select a prearranged church staff member as captain for each group. Have each captain put on a pair of huge long johns (top and bottom, if two pieces) over his or her clothes. The object of the game is to have team members blow up balloons, tie them, and see how many they can stuff inside the long johns of their team captain in three minutes. After yelling "stop," count the number of balloons for each team by popping them while they are still inside the long johns.*

CLOSING

Form a hand-holding circle to include everyone. Place chairs or wheelchairs when necessary.

The leader should comment on the church as an inclusive fellowship of persons who care for each other, both at church and away from the church.

*Adapted from *The Good Times Game Book,* Douglas Kamstra, Compiler (Grand Rapids: Baker Book House, 1981), pp. 10-11.

LEADER: Repeat after me:

The church is here in the midst of us. *(Wait for repetition.)*

We are the church at the playground, school, home, and workplace. *(Wait for repetition.)*

We are the church everywhere through our missionary outreach. *(Wait for repetition.)*

We are the church to the community where we serve. *(Wait for repetition.)*

We are the church. *(Wait for repetition.)*

Sing, "We Are the Church."

EVENT THEME:
HOW THE BIBLE CAME TO US

**A series of related tableaux describes the history of
how the Bible came to us.**

A tableau is the representation of a scene in which actors freeze in action and remain motionless while a narrator tells the story.

SCHEDULE

*Browse Bible collection and get nametags.
*Focus Activity:
   1. Skit, "Where Did the Bible Come From?"
   2. Give directions and go to seven work groups.
   3. Present scenes, "How the Bible Came to Us."
*Closing
   1. Skit, "Answer, Where We Got Our Bible."
*Refreshments.
*Alternate Plan:
   Have a Sunday school class or youth group prepare the tableau scenes ahead of time and make a presentation to the intergenerational group.

ADVANCE PREPARATION

*Reproduce scripts for distribution at planning meetings. Provide scene scripts for each group.
*Select a director (probably Reverend Aston from the introductory skit) for the entire tableaux series, "How the Bible Came to Us." Dramatic experience is not necessary; this person is a facilitator, the one person in charge.
*Recruit actors for introductory and closing skits (the actors are the same), and rehearse. Keep it simple.
*Select a leader for each scene.
*Select a property person or committee.
*Meet with leaders and committees to establish goals and procedures. Stress the importance of demonstrating a big idea rather than a polished

performance. The procedure will depend on the ages and size of your group.

*Decide who will narrate this series. Will it be the overall director, one appointed person, or a representative from each small group? Plan for a standing microphone.

*Plan to bridge the intervals between scenes by singing "The Bible Is a Treasure Book." (See copy of the song at the end of script.) Select a song leader and accompanist, or make a tape of "The Bible Is a Treasure Book" that may be played between scenes.

*Ask participants to bring Bibles from home for a browsing arrangement. Stress labeling all Bibles.

ROOM ARRANGEMENT

*Arrange tables with seating for maximum visibility of the staging area. Put boxes of supplies (scripts, costumes, props) out after the introductory skit.

FOCUS ACTIVITY

WHERE DID THE BIBLE COME FROM?

Production Notes

Characters: David, sixteen years old; Jackson, fifteen years old; Angela, ten years old; Dianne, fourteen years old; Reverend Aston, man or woman, any age.

Properties: A sign that reads "Our Bible," Bibles of several sizes and colors, and a table.

Costumes: Casual dress.

Setting: The hallway of your church. Dianne is making a poster on a table, stage right. David, Jackson, and Angela, each carrying a stack of Bibles, enter stage left.

ANGELA:	*(Drops a Bible)* Hey! Wait!
JACKSON:	*(Stops)* What is it now?
ANGELA:	I dropped one.
DAVID:	*(Turns toward* ANGELA*)* Hurry! Reverend Aston is waiting in the sanctuary for these.
JACKSON:	Here! *(Picks up the Bible and puts it on* ANGELA's *stack)*
DAVID:	Come on, then. *(Moves toward table)*
DIANNE:	*(Holds up the "Our Bible" sign so the audience can read it with her)* Looks great.
	(DAVID, JACKSON, *and* ANGELA *stop to look.*)
DIANNE:	Where *did* the Bible come from anyway?

DAVID, **JACKSON, and** **ANGELA:**	*(In unison)* Room Six.
DIANNE:	I mean where did *the* Bible come from?
	(DAVID, JACKSON, and ANGELA set the Bibles down on the table. Each one shrugs and mumbles indicating, "I don't know.")
DIANNE:	I mean who wrote it? *(Pause)* Was it carved in stone? *(Pause)* Was it written on paper?
	(DAVID, JACKSON, and ANGELA leaf through Bible pages.)
ANGELA:	Yeah, paper.
DIANNE:	I mean the beginning. And was it always in chapters? And why are some Bibles different from others?
	(REVEREND ASTON enters stage right.)
REVEREND ASTON:	Where are the Bibles?
DAVID:	Here, sir.
DIANNE:	*(To REVEREND ASTON)* Reverend Aston, where did the Bible come from?
REVEREND ASTON:	Room Six, I hope.
DIANNE:	No, I mean who wrote it? Where? When?
REVEREND ASTON:	You want a sermon on the spot?
DIANNE:	No. I want you tell me how we got our Bible.
REVEREND ASTON:	Let's ask the audience. They're going to make scenes to show how our Bible came to be. *(To audience)* Here is how our tableau scenes will be put together. You will be divided into tableau work groups with a leader for each group. Your leader will (1) help you read the script for your scene and (2) help you decide how to portray the information for the rest of us. You need not follow the suggested scripted setting for your scene. You need to know that a tableau is a representation of a scene in which the actors walk on stage portraying the action of their script, then freeze in action and remain motionless until the narrator completes the information or story. Props are in the center of the room and may be borrowed for your scene. (Or, your leader has props for your scene.) As you prepare your scene, you will learn the details about one part of the history of how we got our Bible. As each group portrays a scene, you will learn more about the handing down of God's word. When we finish, we will all have a timeline of Bible history.

At this point, introduce the scene leaders and tell the group how they will be divided, and announce the time that the sharing of scenes will begin (about fifteen minutes). A good way to call "time" when you are ready is to play the song "The Bible Is a Treasure Book."

In the midst of what may seem like mass confusion, trust the process. Groups are bonding and learning.

HOW THE BIBLE CAME TO US

SCENE I

SPOKEN RECORDS

Production Notes

Properties: Rugs or blankets. A few stones. Make a transportable fire by arranging pieces of firewood on a twenty-four-by-twenty-four-inch piece of plywood so that they form a nest for a large, standing flashlight that has been covered with red cloth or plastic. Do not cover an electric light with cloth or plastic.

Costumes: Cloaks or robes with belt made from folded lengths of cloth. Sandals.

Setting: A group of ancient Hebrews sits huddled close to a campfire. Children lean against parents, some of them asleep and some playing with stones or fringes on clothing. The storyteller stands by the fire, looks from one person to the other, then freezes in that position. The narrator begins.

NARRATOR: The earliest Bible people didn't settle in cities. Their community was a group of families and friends who moved their entire community to a new location when their sheep had eaten all the grass in one location, or when the water in a stream dried up. Sometimes they moved on when tribes in the area became unfriendly.

Storytelling was a form of recreation as they sat around the campfire after the evening meal. It was also a way of handing down the wisdom of their time to the next generation. Daring adventures were recounted with reverence. Contrasts of the beauty and the hardships of life were told in poetic words that painted vivid pictures in the mind. Often the storyteller told how he felt about the day's events. Sometimes the stories told the origin of something, or recalled a special place. Many times these special stories defined a covenant or agreement between God and his people, and always the stories were told with care.

What we call the oral, or spoken, tradition was a gradual process that took place over many years, but these spoken pictures were transferred centuries later into printed words. They are the story of where we came from—our biblical beginning.

(Music begins. All actors exit stage left as stage is set from right and actors for next scene enter stage right.)

SCENE II

ANCIENT WRITINGS

Production Notes

Properties: A table, a quill (feather), a scroll made from rolled and secured butcher paper, large papier-mâché stones, chisels, blocks of clay, pointed instruments, a piece of leather, a dip pen and ink, broken bits of pottery, a brush, and paint or ink.

Costumes: Dark tunics or robes and sandals.

Setting: Several persons on stage depict the use of ancient writing materials. One person holding a large quill sits at a table on which rests a large scroll. Other persons may sit on the floor or in chairs holding and writing on large stones, clay tablets, pieces of parchment, pieces of leather, a piece of wood, and broken bits of pottery.

(Characters enter stage right and as they freeze on stage, the narrator begins.)

NARRATOR: When people finally started writing down the words that had been told and retold, they used clay tablets, broken bits of pottery, wood, tree bark, and stone. Many of the early laws and commandments were written on stone. Although stone lasted a long, long time, it was too heavy to send someone. Imagine the heavy reading one could get from a stone library.

About three thousand years before Christ, Egyptians learned how to make papyrus (pa-PY-rus) from marsh plants. This provided a flat surface similar to our paper. Soon people in most parts of the world used papyrus. They also used animal skins that were tanned into smooth leather suitable for writing. Later people learned to soak the skins in lime water, scrape off the hair, and stretch the skins to make parchment. These were fastened together to make scrolls. When a scroll became too long, it was continued on a second scroll.

As time went on, bits of oral tradition and pieces of written work about God-inspired persons were woven together to form what is now known as the Books of Law in our Old Testament.

It took many men a thousand years to complete in Hebrew what we know of the Old Testament. But the development of writing materials and the pulling together of stories and scraps of written facts formed the wonderful beginning of the Bible. This awesome story of exciting adventures with God has been preserved for us—often with great difficulty, but always with religious determination. They are our inheritance.

(Music begins. Actors exit stage left as actors and stage setters for scene three enter stage right.)

SCENE III

THE BIBLE IN JESUS' DAY

Production Notes

Properties: A large scroll made from butcher paper that has been taped then rolled onto two wooden-handled rolling pins. Write over the roll with a fine felt tip pen.

Costumes: Sandals, short tunics, skull caps or cloth squares for each child's head. Sandals and a longer tunic or robe for the rabbi.

Setting: A group of children sits on the floor. The boys wear skull caps or squares of cloth on their heads. A rabbi stands in front of the children holding a scroll. As the actors enter stage right to take their places, the narrator reads.

NARRATOR: In Jesus' time, every Jewish community had the parts of our Bible we call the Old Testament. It was handwritten on scrolls in Hebrew. But Jewish common people probably never touched the holy word. Only the priests and scribes could keep and handle the precious holy scrolls because they had been slowly hand copied with great care by persons called scribes. Scribes knew the laws and commandments, and were about the only persons who knew how to read or write.

Selections from the Law and the Prophets were read aloud and discussed in the temple and synagogues. Only Jewish male children attended school. They sat cross legged on the floor while the teacher read a sentence. Then they repeated it all together. In such a setting, Jesus learned scripture and learned to read. As he grew older he was allowed to read from the scrolls in the synagogue.

(Music begins. Actors exit stage left as actors and stage setters for scene four enter stage right.)

SCENE IV

MONKS MAKE COPIES

Production Notes

Properties: Tables, chairs, sheets of paper, quills or dip pens, and a large bound book.

Costumes: Dark robes with hoods.

Setting: Monks are seated on the floor and at tables. Each monk has a quill and several pieces of paper. One monk stands in front and to the side of the stage holding a large, heavy bound book. This person depicts the reader for the copyists. After the monks enter stage right, take their places, and freeze, the narrator begins.

NARRATOR: After Jesus' death, his stories and sayings were passed on in the Aramaic language. However, when this information was written down for the newly formed Christian church, it was written in the language most people spoke, Greek. Scribes copied the holy scrolls, and after the fourth and fifth centuries they began to use vellum, which could be bound into a book.

After the Old Testament and the New Testament were put together as the Bible, the copying was done mostly by monks in monasteries, who devoted their entire lives to keeping alive the good news of the scriptures. Sometimes several monks wrote while one read aloud, but upon many occasions one monk worked alone at the tedious job. Many monks were talented in art and illustrated the scriptures with colored pictures and decorated them with gold.

Sometimes the monk's mind wandered when he became tired, and he made a mistake. Often the mistake was not noticed, but if it was discovered later, the next copyist put a note in the margin to either correct the error or call attention to it. Very few changes were made, however, and the ancient Isaiah scroll that was found near the Dead Sea reads nearly the same as scrolls made hundreds of years earlier. This fact is a tribute to the many men of God who, with great care, preserved for us wonderful records of God's dealings with humankind. Although many mistakes may have been made in the copying and handing down of our Bible, it is really not too surprising to discover that the great ideas and stories of persons and their dealing with God have remained the same for centuries. God guided those who worked.

(Music begins. Actors exit stage left as actors and stage setters for scene five enter stage right.)

SCENE V

HUNGER FOR A READABLE BIBLE

Production Notes

Properties: A cardboard window frame, a Bible, a candle, and any other quickly moveable props suggesting that the scene takes place in an attic.

Costumes: Families dress in fourteenth-century clothing, if available, but contemporary clothing is suitable.

Setting: A group of two families is huddled together in an attic listening to a Lollard priest read the Bible. A lookout is stationed at stage left (or the door) and one at the window. As the actors take their places from stage right, the narrator begins.

NARRATOR: Hunger for a readable Bible caused daring men and women across the years to translate the Bible into their native languages. Martin Luther translated it into German. With dogged determination, many others worked in secret to make the Bible available to the few who could read.

In England, where the Latin Bible was a guarded book upon which only the priesthood could look, there was an enormous hunger for Bible reading. Convinced that the poor of the land needed access to the Bible, John Wycliffe and others worked in secret to translate the entire Bible into English, making all the copies by hand. Wycliffe also organized a band of priests, called the Lollards, who traveled the countryside without pay teaching the poor. They met in secret places, such as the attic shown in our scene, for the wonderful treat of talking about the Bible. Sometimes the Lollards repeated Bible verses, and sometimes they sang the gospel story. Later, as Wycliffe translated the Bible into English, these traveling Bible enthusiasts read from the scriptures. The church, which used only Latin Bibles, punished anyone caught copying the Bible or translating it or holding secret Bible readings.

About this same time the printing press was invented in Germany, and copies of the Bible were slowly made available in other languages. John Wycliffe and his followers did more than translate the Bible into English; they created and nourished a hunger for knowledge of the Bible. As years passed, this enthusiasm for the Bible urged the common people to make demands that led to more Bibles and the right to read them.

(Music begins. Actors exit stage left as stage setters and actors for scene six enter stage right.)

SCENE VI

SURPRISES IN EXCAVATIONS

Production Notes

Properties: Rocks, a large basket of dirt, three or four shovels, a brush, broken pottery, coins, and buttons.

Costumes: Khaki pants, T-shirts, and walking shoes.

Setting: A group of amateur archaeologists—men, women, and children—enter stage right and examine objects that are laid on the ground. Three or four shovels are laid aside. One person leans on a shovel. One person carefully brushes the dirt away from a broken piece of pottery. One person handles a large stone. Others may look at coins or buttons. They freeze as the narrator begins.

NARRATOR: As years passed, the words and bindings of the Bible changed, but the contents remained alive with the spirit of truth. The Bible was translated into hundreds of languages, and as late as the thirteenth century, was divided into chapters. In the fourteenth century it was divided into verses that made it easier to read. New versions of the Bible made meanings clearer.

About this time, scholars who had been studying the words and history of the Bible had a surprise that made them almost jump out of their skins! Archaeologists uncovered cities, homes, and evidences of cultures that gave new clues to understanding the Bible. Coins, bits of pottery, utensils, and records on stone and clay have told them much about people in the Bible and the times in which they lived.

But some clues didn't have to be dug up. A shepherd in Palestine discovered a cave holding ten jars of ancient scrolls, some of them older than our most ancient manuscript. These scrolls, plus the articles dug up by archaeologists, provide background for the history of the Bible and give us more evidence that verifies the details of God's story. And to the surprise of many, these artifacts support the idea that the Bible, although handled by many generations in its writing, has remained trustworthy. The Bible is indestructible, beautiful, accurate and can be believed.

(Music begins. Actors exit stage left as stage setters and actors for scene seven enter stage right.)

SCENE VII

A BIBLE FOR EVERY PERSON

Production Notes

Properties: A shelf or shelves of books. Tables full of an assortment of Bibles and Bible related books. A sign reading "Bookstore."

Costumes: Contemporary clothing.

Setting: Contemporary persons of all ages enter stage right and move around tables of books. The scene freezes when the narrator begins as they pick up Bibles to look at them.

NARRATOR: The average Bible buyer might be confused by the array of Bibles available. Many persons find the story of God's reaching to people a difficult one to understand, and they labor over finding just the right record of it. Honestly, the Bible is not easy to understand, and readers must struggle to make its message useful, as well as beautiful. That is the reason why so many persons for so many centuries have labored to translate the Bible into everyday language.

A bookstore might contain Bibles in several languages and translations—some of them ancient but beautiful. Modern translations reflecting the most recent archaeological findings and modern paraphrases are also featured in book stores. A paraphrase, such as *The Living Bible,* contains verses that have been placed into easy-to-understand words and modern phrases. A student of the Bible, while finding the paraphrases easy to understand, will also want to read from a preferred translation of the Bible that remains true to the most trusted documents.

Choosing a translation is a very personal matter. Catholic readers may prefer *The Jerusalem Bible* or the *New American Bible,* while Jewish readers might prefer the English translation of the Hebrew Scriptures published by the Jewish Publication Society of America.

Young people taking their first steps in scripture may prefer the *Good News Bible* with its simple, direct style. Or they might like the *New English Bible,* which comes across in its readable style as very personal. The *New International Version Study Bible* is also a favorite. Finding the right Bible for your age and inclination is important. There is one for you!

(Music begins. Actors exit stage left as skit members enter stage right.)

SKIT CLOSING FOR TABLEAU

Answer: Where We Got Our Bible

(Enter stage right JACKSON, DAVID, ANGELA, DIANNE, and REVEREND ASTON. *Each carries a Bible.)*

DIANNE: That was a great story.

REVEREND ASTON: Well, answer now, how did the Bible come to us?

DIANNE: From warm campfires on a cold night.

JACKSON: Through stones and scrolls and scraps of dusty paper with faded ink.

ANGELA: Through backache for the copiers and suffering for the translators.

DAVID: Through heavy books and the printing press and smuggled copies read in attics.

REVEREND ASTON: You're all right. The work of many persons brought us the Bible. But the Bible comes to us only if we open the cover and read. Then it becomes our handbook for living.

The Bible Is a Treasure Book

ST. ANNE CM

Elizabeth McE. Shields   Probably by William Croft, 1678-1727

The Bi – ble is a trea – sure book Of
The Bi – ble is a trea – sure book Of
The Bi – ble is a trea – sure book: It

sto – ries that are true: It tells of peo – ple
vers – es old and new: Some make us think of
tells how, long a – go, Christ Je – sus came to

long a – go, Of folks like me and you.
love – ly things; Some show us what to do.
live on earth, Our Fa – ther's love to show.

EVENT THEME: ADVENT

SCHEDULE

*Browse displays and get nametags.
*Serve dinner or refreshments.
*Focus Activity:
   1. Perform the skit, "Uncle Baxter Finally Gets There."
*Small Groups:
   1. Make Advent wreaths or Christmas cards.
   2. Older groups can discuss Christmas expectations.
*Sharing Time:
   Litany and Christmas carols.

ADVANCE PREPARATION

*Recruit a moderator whose job it will be to preside at the meal, introduce The Advent Players, and give all directions for dividing into groups.
*Recruit group leaders, one for each ten to fifteen persons.
*Order (or write your own) Advent worship service booklets. Estimate two for each family.
*Collect supplies for the small group activity you have selected.
*Enlist help for a Christmas display wall, or for taking care of items brought for the needy.
*Select a drama director who will recruit the cast and rehearse skit. (See introduction, p. 5.)

ROOM ARRANGEMENT

*Arrange chairs in fan shaped rows, in front of the staging area.
*Set up tables for making Advent wreaths. Place a set of supplies on each table. (See instructions for making wreaths.)
*After skit, move chairs to prearranged tables. Remember that children cannot sit still in one place for a long period of time. Provide help for persons with handicapping conditions who must move with the group.

AS PEOPLE LEAVE

*Make nametags.
*Browse display wall that has been provided by a Sunday school class or special activity group such as vacation Bible school, or the Boy or Girl Scouts.
*Alternate Activity: Have each family bring Christmas ornaments, food, or clothing for the needy.

FOCUS ACTIVITY

UNCLE BAXTER FINALLY GETS THERE
**When he arrives, Uncle Baxter is not at all
what the Martin family expected.**

Production Notes

Characters: Uncle Baxter, Mother, Father, Tom (fifteen years old), Ardith (ten years old), Jenny (six years old), and the event moderator, who opens and closes the skit and gives directions for moving to the next activity.
Playing Time: 8 minutes
Properties: A table, a red tablecloth, an Advent wreath, candles, matches, a Bible, six chairs, one upholstered chair, a small shopping bag with yo-yo and jacks, a window (can be painted on posterboard and hung on wall), an Advent booklet, a newspaper, and noise for a ringing phone.
Costumes: All wear dressy clothes except Uncle Baxter, who wears baggy pants and old faded clothing.
Setting: The Martin family den, in the evening. Next to a window, stage right, is a comfortable, upholstered chair. Left of center stage is a table covered with a red cloth. On the table is an Advent wreath, candles, and a Bible. Arranged to the back and sides of the table are six chairs. Chairs may be omitted and characters can stand around the table.

> *(ARDITH enters and stands by the window looking out, presenting a profile to the audience.* TOM *enters playing with a yo-yo and stands stage left.* JENNY, *carrying jacks or a puzzle, enters with* MOTHER *and* FATHER, *sits on floor to play.* MOTHER *arranges and rearranges the Advent table.* FATHER *sits in a chair reading a newspaper. Characters freeze as* MODERATOR *makes the introduction, and unfreeze when* MODERATOR *sits down.)*

MODERATOR: We present The Advent Players in "Uncle Baxter Finally Gets There." All preparations have been made for the Martin family's annual Christmas Eve family worship service and dinner, but Uncle Baxter has not arrived. *(Sits in audience)*

MOTHER: Stop looking out the window every two seconds. You're making me nervous.

ARDITH: *(Turning toward* MOTHER*)* But where is he? Uncle Baxter said he would be here by six o'clock, and it's eight o'clock now. Where is he?

MOTHER: He must have been delayed. Important people are very busy.

TOM: *(Continues with yo-yo)* Yeah! Spending money.

ARDITH: I hope he's spending it on us. Did you make space under the Christmas tree for his gifts?

TOM: Yeah, I cleared a huge spot.

FATHER: *(Puts paper down)* Now don't expect too much from Uncle Baxter. Gifts or not, we must welcome him. I just want him to feel comfortable.

JENNY: *(Sarcastic)* He should be comfortable. After all he has the best chair in the house, and you moved the color television into his room.

TOM: That's *my* room, which I vacated by force. At least my bed got a new bedspread and silk sheets. Why can't we all sleep on silk sheets?

MOTHER: We don't need them. Uncle Baxter is accustomed to luxury, and we want him to feel right at home.

FATHER: *(Rises and goes to window)* If you ask me, we're trying to make him think we're something we aren't.

MOTHER: Oh now, Martin, you know we aren't showing off.

FATHER: Then why are we using the silver tonight? And why are we having steak?

ARDITH: Mom says he's accustomed.

JENNY: Yeah, accustomed.

TOM: And he's powerful. Almost like a king. When he speaks, people jump.

FATHER: Not me. I remember when we were kids, he always sneaked into my bedroom during a thunderstorm, scared to death.

JENNY: Really?

MOTHER: Oh, come on, he has changed. He's not afraid, and he's powerful.

ARDITH: Do you think he'll have a limousine and driver?

JENNY: And what will we do with the driver? Where can he sleep?

MOTHER: I'm sure Baxter has made arrangements. He's very efficient.

TOM: If he's so efficient, why is he two-and-a-half hours late for dinner?

MOTHER: His plane from Paris was probably late. Could be very late. Let's go ahead with our family Christmas Eve service. We can eat when he comes.

(Everyone agrees, saying "Good idea," "All right," or "Yeah!" They all move to the Advent table. FATHER opens the Bible. MOTHER dims the lights. The family gathers behind and beside the Advent table, facing stage front.)

TOM: *(Lights one candle on the wreath)* This candle is lighted to remind us that many people had been looking for and waiting for the birth of Jesus. They were expecting a Messiah. This candle represents hope.

ARDITH: *(Helps JENNY light second candle)* Now we light the second candle. It reminds us that Mary and Joseph had a baby that grew up to show people about love.

JENNY: It's the candle of love.

MOTHER: *(Lights a candle)* This candle will remind us of the beautiful announcement of Jesus' birth made by the angels long ago. It represents wonder and singing.

ARDITH: *(Lights a candle)* I light the fourth candle to represent the joy we feel as we celebrate the birth of Jesus.

FATHER: Let's sing "Joy to the World." *(They begin singing. In the middle of the first verse JENNY runs to the window.)*

JENNY: I hear a car! He's here!

(Everyone runs to look out the window)

JENNY: I don't believe it!

ARDITH: Believe what? *(peers around JENNY)*

JENNY: He's driving a bashed-in Volkswagen. Look, there by the yard light.

ARDITH: I thought rich men had limousines and drivers.

(UNCLE BAXTER knocks on the door. FATHER exits stage left and returns with UNCLE BAXTER. They shake hands. UNCLE BAXTER carries a small shopping bag.)

FATHER: Great to see you.

UNCLE BAXTER: You look fantastic! *(Inspects other family members)* So, this is your family. *(Glances at the lighted candles)* Oh, am I interrupting something?

MOTHER: We were just starting our Christmas Eve service. It's something we do every year.

UNCLE BAXTER: Well, you go right ahead while I make a phone call. I'll be right back. Point me to the phone.

FATHER: *(Points out stage left)* It's right down the hall.

(UNCLE BAXTER exits stage left, and everyone goes back to the Advent celebration.)

MOTHER:	Well, I never! Can't he stop talking to his stockbroker just once?
TOM:	Let's get on with the service so we can get to the food.
ARDITH:	*(Reads from a booklet)* As Isaiah told everyone it would happen, people waited years for a messiah. When he came they called him wonderful, counselor, almighty, the prince of peace. *(Hands the booklet to* TOM*)*
TOM:	*(Reads)* But many were expecting a king who would rule with justice and could make the conditions of their lives better. They were surprised when the baby who was born grew up to be a servant to humankind who told them new things about what God was like. He wanted to be a spiritual ruler, to rule people's hearts, not a kingdom.
UNCLE BAXTER:	*(Enters from left)* Sorry to interrupt. Go right ahead. *(Takes an empty seat.)*
MOTHER:	We were ready for the litany. Everyone responds "There is joy in Christmas" after Martin says a sentence.
UNCLE BAXTER:	Okay.
FATHER:	We sing and get ready for Christmas in our hearts.
ALL:	There is joy in Christmas.
FATHER:	We sing and give thanks for Jesus' birth.
ALL:	There is joy in Christmas.
FATHER:	We sing and give thanks for the Bible where we can read about Jesus.
ALL:	There is . . .
	(The phone rings.)
UNCLE BAXTER:	*(Rising)* That will be for me. Sorry. *(Exits left)*
FATHER:	*(Pounds fist on table)* He is about to ruin everything. Why can't he forget money for once and just be family?
MOTHER:	All the preparations, and he didn't notice.
TOM:	Powerful people are always like that. We studied it in sociology. They think the world revolves about themselves. They never consider anyone else.
ARDITH:	I'm really disappointed. Did you notice he has only a little shopping bag full of presents? I thought he would bring lots of expensive presents.
JENNY:	Shh. He'll hear you. Let's be nice to him.
	(UNCLE BAXTER enters from door.)
UNCLE BAXTER:	*(Looking sad)* Sorry to interrupt.
EVERYONE CHORUS:	It's okay. All right.

UNCLE BAXTER:	I always get carried away with the spirit of Christmas. Sometimes it frazzles me.
MOTHER:	*(Showing her disgust a little)* Us, too.
UNCLE BAXTER:	I own an orphanage in New York, and I try never to be away from the children at Christmas.
FATHER:	So that's why you never accept our Christmas invitations!
UNCLE BAXTER:	*(Sits down)* It's not that I haven't wanted to come, but so many people depend on me. And, of all things, when I called there earlier, the house father said the plumbing had gone bad and the Christmas tree and all the presents got wet. I guess the children will have a sorry Christmas.
MOTHER:	I hope everything dries out before morning.
UNCLE BAXTER:	Not much chance. There will be some very last minute shopping.
FATHER:	*(Looks at watch)* It's already very late.
UNCLE BAXTER:	That last call was bad news, too. Would you mind doing one thing for me right here in the middle of your service?
	(They all look at each other and shrug a sort of "What's next?" shrug.)
UNCLE BAXTER:	Would you mind praying with me for a friend in Philadelphia? My friend has taken a turn for the worse.
JENNY:	We didn't think you'd be the praying type.
MOTHER:	Shh.
UNCLE BAXTER:	Why not?
ARDITH:	*(Hesitantly)* I have to tell you, Uncle Baxter, that you aren't what we expected. Instead of a rich business mogul busy with his stockbroker, we got a real person who is more interested in people and prayer than power. *(Pauses)* But I'm glad you came.
JENNY:	Me, too.
FATHER:	Seems like that's the way it was with Jesus' coming. He wasn't what anyone expected. Just better.
TOM:	I'm glad you came, too. But will you please get on with the prayer so we can get to the steak? I'm starving.
UNCLE BAXTER:	Let's hold hands to pray.
	(They hold hands in a circle as the room lights come on.)
MODERATOR:	*(Standing)* Thank you, Advent Players. *(Leads in applause then continues)* The Jews had been expecting a messiah for years. When he came quietly in the form of a baby, they weren't quite ready for him, and they had to change their ideas about who he was and what kind of ruler he would be. Sometimes we are like that in our understanding of

Jesus. And sometimes we are like that in getting ready for
Christmas. Tonight we will prepare a family wreath that
will help remind us to get our hearts ready for Christmas.

At this point, explain the purpose of your selected activity and tell how the
activity will be accomplished. Groups will remain together until each one has
completed the closing litany. Give instructions for dividing into groups of
ten to fifteen.

SMALL GROUPS

How to make an Advent wreath

Each group leader should have supplies ready at his or her table. Family
units (may be from one to seven persons) will each construct a wreath that
consists of a base (large Styrofoam block or wood with five candle-sized holes
drilled in each piece), four red or white candles and one purple candle, and
decorations for the base, which may be ribbon, plastic holly, or glitter. Do not
use natural greenery, as it is a fire hazard.

Directions: Write the family name on the bottom of the base. Let each
family decide how to decorate the base from the supplies on hand. Insert
candles. Give each family two Advent worship service books. Advent
worship service booklets are available from most religious book stores.

If you wish to write your own worship service, remember that simplicity is
the key for worshiping with young children. The candles are symbols: joy,
hope, love, expectation, promise, and light. They are found in the coming of
Christ story: Matthew 2:1-12; Isaiah 9:2, 6, 7; and Luke 2:1-20.

ALTERNATE ACTIVITIES

1. Make Christmas or Advent cards using a candle design. Talk about the
   meaning of Advent as you work.
2. If this event is for youth or adults, discuss personal expectations of
   Christmas. Lead into personal thoughts by discussing the skit:
   a. Which character placed most value on things?
   b. What can you plan to do during Advent to emphasize the value of
      people more than the value of things?
   c. How will you know if *things* are becoming too important to you?
   d. Time spent by candlelight or by the soft glow of Christmas lights can
      be relaxing and joyous, but many families encounter trouble getting
      everyone together. How can this problem be overcome?
   e. What do you personally expect from the contemporary event of
      Christmas? Are you being realistic? Is your focus in line with Christ's
      teachings?

CLOSING LITANY

Compliment groups on the joyful work and lovely wreaths. Give
instructions for the group to respond "Thank you, God" as you indicate in
the litany. Light some candles.

LEADER:	As we stand by the candles, we give thanks to God for the gift of his son, Jesus.
GROUP:	Thank you, God.
LEADER:	We give thanks for the spirit of friendship and peace that we feel during the Christmas season.
GROUP:	Thank you, God.
LEADER:	We give thanks for Jesus who showed us how to love others.
GROUP:	Thank you, God.
LEADER:	Amen.

(Softly sing Christmas carols children know.)

EVENT THEME: CHRISTMAS GIFTS

Not all gifts are tied up with ribbons.

The drama for this event, "No Ribbons on Boxes," is about a teenage girl with a blended family and extended gift-giving problems; a backstage Magi; and the shared Christmas memories of a Jewish actor and a lonely woman. The play is about gift-giving, but might be used for an event dealing with the changing of rituals in divorced families.

SCHEDULE

*Get nametags.
*Get Together Activity:
  1. Bring cookies to share.
  2. Eat some of the cookies with punch.
  3. Pack boxes of cookies to take to lonely persons.
*Focus Activity:
  1. Play: "No Ribbons on Boxes."
*Sharing Time
  1. Informal gathering after the play.
  2. (Optional) Discuss the play from a point-of-view perspective.

ADVANCE PREPARATION

*Plan for nametags.
*Select an event moderator.
*Designate a cookie chairperson.
*Recruit a refreshments chairperson.
*Select a play director.
*Select and train discussion leaders.

ROOM ARRANGEMENT

*A table for nametags.
*A refreshment area.

*Tables with boxes for packing cookies.
*Chairs arranged around a staging area.

AS PEOPLE ARRIVE

*Get nametags.
*Hand over cookies to designated cookie person.
*As cookies arrive, eat refreshments.
*Have the moderator explain the purpose of packing boxes of cookies. The cookies are to be delivered by individuals (not by a committee) who demonstrate appropriate love and concern.

FOCUS ACTIVITY

NO RIBBONS ON BOXES
A play about a teenage girl with extended gift-giving problems, a backstage Magi, and shared Christmas memories.

Production Notes

Characters: Peggy (twelve or thirteen years old); Babs Benedict, Peggy's glamorous stage star mother; Gustav Beck, a well-known Shakespearean actor, (in his mid-fifties), co-star of Babs Benedict; Mrs. Bentley (fifty to sixty), the aloof, grouchy executive director of the stage play in which Babs Benedict and Gustav Beck are appearing; Nelson, a somewhat clumsy eighteen-year-old backstage helper, errand person, and would-be actor.
Playing time: 25-30 minutes.
Properties:
Scene I: Set backstage in a Broadway theater. You will need a telephone, desk with chair, papers and boxes for the desk, a tall green plant, a long wooden bench with a back, water and dispenser, a door with a star on it and name Babs Benedict, trunks containing warm clothing, blankets, pillows, and rugs, old stage scenery and/or boxes, an old lamp, a standard florescent camping lamp, a McDonald's hamburger sack, a candle in a holder, and paper containing Peggy's long Christmas list.
Scene II: Set the same as scene I except that it is dark. The trunks have been pulled to center stage to create a warm nest for persons trapped in the studio. In addition, you will need a telephone, sacks of potato chips, empty cookie cartons, empty soft drink cans, a battery powered lantern, a candle in a holder, and trunks with contents from scene I. Scissors and a three-foot artificial Christmas tree in its own stand are offstage right.
Sound: Telephone.
Costumes:
Scene I: Peggy—sweater and pants, heavy coat, boots, scarf, purse;
Gustav—long, rich looking robe, dress shoes, a velvet cloak with a fur collar and jeweled clasp;

Babs—large chenille robe, towel or turban for her head, full skirt, blouse, flat heeled shoes;

Mrs. Bentley—business suit, high heeled shoes;

Nelson—uniform of stage staff, that is matching twill pants and shirt, work shoes.

Scene II: Peggy—Magi's cloak from scene I over heavy winter clothing;

Gustav—Magi's robe under a turtle neck sweater, a man's overcoat, man's early American nightcap;

Babs—a man's suit with heavy wool neck scarf over her head;

Mrs. Bentley—fur coat and fur ear muffs over her business suit;

Nelson—wears his uniform, leather gloves, a ski mask, and adds a long shepherd's cloak from a trunk.

Setting: The backstage of a theater. Along the right wall is Mrs. Bentley's desk with a chair. The desk is piled with papers and boxes. Upstage right corner is a tall, green plant. Next to it upstage are, from stage right to left, a water dispenser, a table on which rests a telephone, a bench with a back, and Babs Benedict's dressing room door. Behind the bench is a bulletin or chalk board with rehearsal dates posted for *The Madison Avenue Magi.* Stage left, stacked neatly, is an assortment of boxes and old scenery flats, two trunks, an old lantern, and a standard florescent camping lamp.

> *(At opening* PEGGY *is setting on the bench.* GUSTAV *is getting a drink from the water dispenser.* MRS. BENTLEY *enters stage right, moves toward her desk, notices* PEGGY, *and stops.)*

MRS. BENTLEY:	*(Coolly)* Are you still here?
PEGGY:	Yes.
GUSTAV:	You can see she's here. What a dumb question.
MRS. BENTLEY:	Listen, Gustav Beck, don't call me dumb. I make out your check.
GUSTAV:	Okay. You're smart.
MRS. BENTLEY:	If *you* were smart, you wouldn't be here. Rehearsal ended at 5:00.
GUSTAV:	You're here!
MRS. BENTLEY:	*(Extreme sarcasm) I'm* not a big shot actor.
GUSTAV:	*(Turns to* PEGGY*)* We won't mind her, honey, she's always grumpy the day before a dress rehearsal.
PEGGY:	I don't mind. It's frown day anyway.
GUSTAV:	Frown day?
MRS. BENTLEY:	What on earth is frown day?
PEGGY:	The cook was frowning this morning. Chased me out of the kitchen. The bus driver frowned at everyone on the bus, and they frowned back. *(She sighs and leans back on the bench.)*
GUSTAV:	Poor kid.
MRS. BENTLEY:	Hurumph! That happens every day on the bus.

(MRS. BENTLEY turns her full attention to the stacks of paperwork on her desk with her back to the audience.)

PEGGY: Then I slipped on the ice and spilled my purse.

GUSTAV: Ice?

PEGGY: It's sleeting outside.

GUSTAV: *(Sits on the bench near Peggy)* What are you doing out on such an afternoon?

PEGGY: Waiting for my mom. *(Points to the door behind her)*

GUSTAV: You mean Babs Benedict?

PEGGY: No, I mean I'm waiting for Mrs. Benedict, my mother.

GUSTAV: *(Sits on bench next to Peggy)* Well darlin', you'll have a long wait. She's having a costume remade. I know. I stood in line at wardrobe to leave my cloak for repair.

PEGGY: She said she'd be out soon.

GUSTAV: Then she will.

PEGGY: That was an hour ago.

GUSTAV: Why don't you go down to the snack bar and have a hot chocolate?

PEGGY: I might miss her. She promised to take me Christmas shopping this afternoon.

GUSTAV: You could go another day.

PEGGY: She said today.

GUSTAV: Well, at least you can go home together.

PEGGY: I have to catch the 5:30 bus home.

GUSTAV: Just wait and go with Babs.

PEGGY: She lives with Roger and I live with Lucy and Daddy.

GUSTAV: Oh.

PEGGY: And they don't like each other very much.

GUSTAV: Oh.

PEGGY: And Lucy won't take me shopping. She's an executive. People do *for* her not *with* her. Not that I don't like her or anything. She just doesn't have time for . . . for me.

GUSTAV: Oh.

PEGGY: That's why she said Mother could take me shopping. Besides, Mother gives me more money to buy things.

GUSTAV: Oh.

PEGGY: And Mother knows how to buy for boys. Last year I got four instant brothers, and had to buy presents for them.

GUSTAV: Oh. Well, I'm sure you selected just the right thing.

PEGGY:	No. Lucy said Mother had terrible taste.
GUSTAV:	Selecting exactly the right gift is always difficult.
PEGGY:	Mother said she would help me buy for Grandma and Grandpa Nelson and Grandma and Grandpa Mitchell and Grandma and Grandpa Benedict and Grandma and Grandpa Ellison. I'm Ellison, by the way. And Great Grandma Marvin. Also, I now have seventeen aunts and uncles. What do you think I should give them?
GUSTAV:	How about Christmas cards?
PEGGY:	Not that simple. It has to be personal. Gifts are a statement about yourself. *(She gets up, paces up and down in front of bench)*
GUSTAV:	Where did you hear that?
PEGGY:	Mother. That's why I need Mother to help me.
GUSTAV:	At least it won't be hard to buy for your father.
PEGGY:	Which one?
GUSTAV:	The one you live with.
PEGGY:	Mother says I have to buy Roger something that costs the same. I can't afford two popcorn poppers.
MRS. BENTLEY:	*(Whispering without turning around)* Get your mother to help you pay for it. Her last play was a smash hit, and at Broadway box office prices she can afford to help you.
PEGGY:	Will the new play bring in lots of money?
MRS. BENTLEY:	*(With authority)* It will.
GUSTAV:	Because she says so.
PEGGY:	What's the new play?
GUSTAV:	*The Madison Avenue Magi.*
PEGGY:	A Christmas play?
GUSTAV:	Yes.
PEGGY:	About the three kings?
GUSTAV:	Just one king. It's really Magi number one.
	(PEGGY sits down next to GUSTAV on the bench.)
PEGGY:	Is it about going to Bethlehem?
GUSTAV:	No. It's about a biblical wise man going to visit the vice president of a finance company, your mother. She plays an honest stockbroker.
PEGGY:	I'm glad she's honest.
GUSTAV:	Except she doesn't make the company enough money. One of the owners of the company tells her to do something illegal. When she refuses, her boss says to become a team player or look for another position after

Christmas. The woman is very depressed until the Magi comes to . . .

(The door opens and BABS stands quietly listening. She wears a towel around her head and a dressing gown. She opens her mouth to speak to PEGGY, then decides to listen.)

PEGGY: *(Interrupting)* I get depressed at Christmas, too.

GUSTAV: Oh?

PEGGY: Nothing is the same anymore.

GUSTAV: Oh.

PEGGY: My sister, Susan, and I always decorated the tree.

GUSTAV: You can still do that.

PEGGY: No. The *court* said I did that last year. This year the *court* says I have to decorate the tree with four boys who treat me like a baby.

GUSTAV: How about decorating the tree with Susan and then spending Christmas with your Father?

PEGGY: Susan's going skiing with Roger and Mother.

GUSTAV: Poor kid. Coming from a divorced family must be tough.

PEGGY: It's nothing. Divorced kids have to keep a stiff lip. They say things like, "That's all right," and "Who cares?" instead of saying "Don't do that to me," and "I love you, don't pull away." It's the divorce rule.

GUSTAV: You're a smart kid. Why do you say what you don't mean?

PEGGY: You either speak your mind, and everyone hates you, or you play happy and your parents still want to see you.

(BABS goes back into her dressing room and quietly closes the door.)

GUSTAV: A difficult thing to do. You're brave.

PEGGY: Most of my friends have the same problem.

GUSTAV: I guess nothing's perfect.

(MRS. BENTLEY turns around and watches with new interest, almost compassion. GUSTAV and PEGGY sit quietly a few seconds.)

PEGGY: What do you do at Christmas time?

GUSTAV: I play Santa Claus.

PEGGY: All the time?

GUSTAV: When I'm not rehearsing.

PEGGY: Doesn't your family want you home at Christmas?

GUSTAV: My wife and I work around our own holiday. I'm Jewish. This year Chanukah is December 23.

(MRS. BENTLEY again busies herself with paperwork at the desk. NELSON enters stage left carrying a long, heavy cloak decorated with fur and jeweled buttons.)

NELSON:	Hey, Mr. Beck! Wardrobe sent this for you to try.
GUSTAV:	*(GUSTAV takes the robe)* Thanks, Nelson.
NELSON:	It had better work. They locked up and left.
PEGGY:	Oh, it's beautiful.

(PEGGY stands, runs her hand around the soft fur collar. MRS. BENTLEY turns around again to look, not rising from her chair.)

NELSON:	By the way, Ben said to lock the door when we leave.
MRS. BENTLEY:	What happened to him?
NELSON:	He took the last bus out.
MRS. BENTLEY:	What does that mean?
NELSON:	Ben heard the buses would stop at 5:30.
PEGGY:	What?
NELSON:	Lots of accidents. One pile up on the bridge killed four people and sent a bunch to the hospital.
PEGGY:	Oh, no! Susan will kill me.
MRS. BENTLEY:	Don't exaggerate. No one will kill you. We will all stay here together until the roads improve. Then we can take a taxi.

(GUSTAV doesn't hear. He puts on the robe and is immediately lost in his part. He turns himself toward the audience, arranging his long cloak behind him.)

NELSON:	Who are you this time, Mr. Beck?
GUSTAV:	I'm the wise man who rode to see the baby Jesus.
NELSON:	*(to PEGGY)* Last time he was King Lear.
GUSTAV:	*(Trying out his voice)* It was a mistake to go . . . *(Starts over with more resonance)* It was a mistake to go to Jerusalem. *(He rearranges his stance.)* We should have waited for the star to reappear without inquiring about it.

(MRS. BENTLEY looks at GUSTAV and snorts with disgust, then shakes her head. NELSON sits on the bench next to PEGGY and, admiringly, they watch the performance.)

GUSTAV:	We should have waited for the star to reappear. And when that cruel, conniving old Herod sent for us, we should have been out—o . . . u . . . t—out, period. *(Pauses to adjust the fastening on his cloak)* He asked us to find the new ruler and report back to him so he could go and worship. Huh! He sneered when he said the word *worship*. We didn't believe him for a minute. But we valued our necks.

(Loosens his fur collar and feels his neck) So we agreed, and went our way. *(Striding back and forth in front of* NELSON *and* PEGGY *with profile to audience)* The star led us to Bethlehem, and we found a beautiful pink baby in a scratchy, smelly manger in a rundown cave. In that setting, how could a baby affect us so? Melchior wept. Caspar knelt so long his arthritic knee froze, and we had to help him up. He limped for days. I . . . I just stood there filled with awe, too touched to move. *(Steps back a few steps as out of the experience)* We considered what to do, arguing all night. What method would Herod use to kill us if we didn't report? Again and again we pitted good against evil, tempted to go back to Herod. *(Steps forward again)* But the baby, the beautiful baby had affected us, so that we could never be the same.

(The lights flicker as BABS, *unnoticed, quietly looks out the dressing room door. She is dressed in a blouse, full skirt, flat heeled shoes. Her hair is combed. She watches a moment and retreats, leaving the door open.)*

GUSTAV: We argued ourselves into a balancing act: good and evil, evil and good. Finally, the dream helped us. We fled.

*(*BABS *quietly reappears in the doorway with a lighted candle and a white McDonald's sack. She places them on the floor at* GUSTAV'S *feet, and sits down next to them.* GUSTAV *looks surprised but talks on.)*

GUSTAV: Ratsudi, my camel, complained all the way out of the territory. He was hungry and tired from the long journey to Bethlehem. I just patted his neck and told him to think of history. "In a hundred years," I told him, "people will remember the baby Jesus. By then no one will remember us, but we did the right thing." *(Sits on the floor across the candle from* BABS.) Caspar's knees got well, and four days later I fed Ratsudi and put him out to rest. But for years I looked behind every bush and into every shadow for the uniformed messenger from Herod. He was a vengeful man not likely to forget.

*(*GUSTAV *takes an imaginary hamburger from the sack, unwraps it, hands it to* BABS, *unwraps one for himself, and begins to eat.* BABS *does not eat.)*

GUSTAV: Come on. It's a triple with cheese.

BABS: *(Shaking her head no)* How did you know? How did you know for certain what to do?

GUSTAV: It was a spiritual choice. *(He pauses)* Then there was something else.

BABS: What?

GUSTAV: It's very personal.

BABS: Tell me.

GUSTAV: Not going back to Herod was a . . . a sort of . . . sort of birthday gift. The gold and spices didn't seem enough. I had to give him a greater gift.

BABS: Oh.

GUSTAV: Oh, what?

BABS: Oh, it *was* a big gift.

GUSTAV: Probably the biggest gift I ever gave anyone.

BABS: All those years when you looked over your shoulder for Herod's men, what did your family think about Herod's men when they went down a dark street? Or did you have a family?

GUSTAV: Eight wives and thirty-one children at the time! Astrology had its ups and downs, but I prospered. And my family . . . they hadn't seen the cruelty in Herod, so they didn't fear the shadows as I did.

BABS: So your family was all right.

GUSTAV: Yes.

BABS: That settles it.

GUSTAV: Settles what?

BABS: I'm leaving the firm of Blocking, Money, and Smitt! *(Pause)* What a weight off my shoulders. Suddenly I'm hungry. *(Takes an imaginary bite of hamburger)*

GUSTAV: Hold on now. You can't just ride your camel out of the executive suite and live happily ever after.

BABS: But my integrity is at stake.

GUSTAV: Corporate integrity takes more than a camel. You can't just pick up and disappear.

MRS. BENTLEY: What can I do?

GUSTAV: Fight!

BABS: Then help me plan my strategy, Mr. . . . Mr. What is your name?

     (The lights flicker again)

GUSTAV: The Magi.

BABS: Don't you have a name?

GUSTAV: I don't bandy it around.

BABS: If we're going to plan corporate strategy, and argue good and evil, then maybe I should call you something.

GUSTAV:	My thirty-one children called me Dad.
BABS:	I'm not your child.
GUSTAV:	Okay, okay. My name is Balthasar.
BABS:	*(Laughing)* I wouldn't bandy that one around either.

(BABS *and* GUSTAV *break their poses, rise, leaving the candle, and hug each other.)*

BABS:	Well done, Bathasar. I love it when you ride in off Madison Avenue on your camel and fill my office with goodness. Every time I play that section, I believe integrity will always win.
GUSTAV:	It must be the cloak. Makes me look official. And I *love* wearing a cloak. *(Swirls the cloak around himself.)*

(NELSON, PEGGY, *and* MRS. BENTLEY *applaud and say "wonderful, touching, great, inspiring."* BABS *and* GUSTAV *bow to their backstage audience. The lights flicker and go out. Only the candle's glow lights the stage. The telephone rings.* MRS. BENTLEY *answers it.)*

MRS. BENTLEY:	Backstage six. Estelle Bentley speaking. Yes. Yes. But she is here. She's safe. *(Turning to* PEGGY) It's Lucy, for you. *(Hands phone to* PEGGY)
PEGGY:	Yes. *(Listens)* I'm sorry, Lucy. *(Pauses)* But they're nice people. No, I didn't do this on purpose. The buses aren't running because of ice on the roads. You just don't understand . . . I . . . *(Whispers)* oh, well.

Scene II

Time: Two hours later.

Setting: Same backstage. Boxes and trunks have been pulled forward to the middle of the stage to form a half-circle backdrop for pillows. In front of this rests a burning oil lamp and the lighted candle from scene I. Soft drink cans, cookie wrappers and bags of potato chips are piled to the right of the oil lamp. Mrs. Bentley, dressed in a fur coat and ear muffs, sits stiffly in a chair, apart from the half-circle of pillows, stage left, barely within the ring of light from the oil lamp. Peggy and Babs are spotlighted standing apart, facing each other, downstage right. They converse as silent action between Gustav and Nelson continues behind them. Gustav is leaning into a trunk. He bobs up and down holding first a blanket, then a pillow, then other items from the trunk. He is dressed in the Magi robe over the turtle neck sweater and under a man's overcoat. A man's early American nightcap dangles from his head to his waist. He finds a shepherd's colorful cloak that he throws to Nelson who puts it on over his jacket and ski mask.

PEGGY:	*(Shoving her gift list at* BABS) You *promised* to help me buy all these gifts.

BABS: I'm sorry that it didn't work out.

PEGGY: Sorry!

BABS: Yes.

PEGGY: Sorry doesn't help me decide what to give everyone.

BABS: I didn't plan the ice storm.

PEGGY: *(Angrily)* You didn't have time to shop with *me*. We had a date at five o'clock! *(Softer, more thoughtfully)* Now it's three days until Christmas and no gifts at all.

BABS: Why did you leave it until the last minute?

PEGGY: So you could help me. Don't you want to shop with me?

BABS: Depends on why you wanted help. I don't think you wanted to be with me while shopping. You wanted my money.

PEGGY: NO. NO.

BABS: What then?

PEGGY: You're the one who said a gift makes a statement about the giver.

BABS: Yes.

PEGGY: I don't know what statement to make.

BABS: Oh, my.

PEGGY: Well?

BABS: Wait a minute. Let me think.

PEGGY: Well?

BABS: Selecting a little something that says, "I love you enough to give you this." That's a statement.

PEGGY: I don't.

BABS: Don't what?

PEGGY: Love them enough to give them anything. I didn't ask for four brothers.

BABS: You hate them that much?

PEGGY: I don't hate them.

BABS: You like them a little?

PEGGY: Sort of.

BABS: Buy a little something, and sign it, "I like you." That's honest.

PEGGY: I'll think about it.

BABS: And . . .

PEGGY: And what?

BABS: What will you do for Lucy?

PEGGY:	I don't know what I'll buy her. I really like her. *(Wistfully)* But she's too busy to notice me.
BABS:	*(BABS takes a long stride closer to* PEGGY*)* I'm sorry.
NELSON:	*(Calling)* Look at the covers we found. Come huddle and warm up.
BABS:	*(Calling back)* Just a minute. *(To* PEGGY*)* Thanks.
PEGGY:	For what?
BABS:	I believe that for once you said what you really wanted to. Sometimes I think you talk through a filter that says, "This is the way divorced kids are supposed to talk." We just had our first honest conversation in a long time.
PEGGY:	*(Meets* BAB's *arms in a hug)* It feels good.
GUSTAV:	Hug over here where it's warmer.
	(GUSTAV tosses a pillow into the circle. It's passing causes the candle to flicker and go out.)
MRS. BENTLEY:	Now look what you've done.
NELSON:	Oh, well, we should save the candle in case the lamp burns out.
	(GUSTAV and NELSON *raise an Indian rug allowing* BABS *to sit next to* NELSON. PEGGY *sits on the other side of* BABS, *closest to* MRS. BENTLEY *sitting in her chair. The phone rings.)*
PEGGY:	Lucy! Not again. I've explained it over and over.
MRS. BENTLEY:	Let me talk to her this time. *(*MRS. BENTLEY *goes to the telephone)*
MRS. BENTLEY:	Backstage six. Yes. She is here. *(Her voice becomes syrupy sweet)* Mrs. Ellison, I know how worried you must be . . . I'd feel that way, too. My daughter was once stranded on a streetcar all night, and I was very worried. What? Let me tell you our situation. The power is off, but we're warm, and we just ate dinner from the snack bar. Who am I? The executive producer. I am a woman of character and will take care of your daughter. Tell her what? *(Voice softening)* Why yes, certainly. And by the way, don't be alarmed if you can't get through to us later. Some of our phones are out. Goodnight. *(Hangs up, calls to the group)* Have all of you contacted your families?
GUSTAV:	Yes.
NELSON:	Hours ago.
BABS:	Yes.
MRS. BENTLEY:	Good. *(She unplugs the phone, and returns to the lighted circle.)* Your stepmother sent a message, Peggy.

PEGGY:	Oh, sure. Don't speak to any strangers and don't have a good time.
MRS. BENTLEY:	*(Softly)* She said to tell you she loves you.
PEGGY:	Her exact words?
MRS. BENTLEY:	*(Her old sarcastic self again)* I said so. *(Sits back in her chair)*
PEGGY:	Wow! That's the first time ever!

(BABS hugs PEGGY and smiles her congratulations.)

NELSON:	It's a lot warmer in our nest, Mrs. Bentley. Why don't you come sit with us?
MRS. BENTLEY:	I'm fine, thank you.

(Everyone settles into the warmest position and is very quiet.)

BABS:	Who will share a childhood Christmas memory?

(No one offers.)

BABS:	Then I'll start. I remember the year my father came home from the war in Italy. He was on crutches, but he was alive. We sat all day Christmas just talking and looking at each other. We were very happy.
PEGGY:	Did he bring you gifts?
BABS:	*(Thoughtfully)* You know, since I was only four years old, I really don't remember. I would say probably.
PEGGY:	Funny you don't remember about gifts.
BABS:	Gifts weren't the memory.
PEGGY:	Who's next?

(No one answers. GUSTAV opens a bag of potato chips, takes some and passes them around. PEGGY rises, takes the two steps to MRS. BENTLEY, gives her some potato chips, then sits back with the group.)

GUSTAV:	Mrs. Bentley, if you'd move into our group, Peggy wouldn't have to get cold coming to you.
MRS. BENTLEY:	I'm fine, thank you.
PEGGY:	What's your memory, Nelson?

(NELSON stands to the side of the small group, rolls up his ski mask so his face is visible.)

NELSON:	Is this my good side? *(Tilts chin up and down and turns head)* I'm practicing for King Lear in a few years.
GUSTAV:	Keep studying, Nelson. You'll make it.
NELSON:	I remember being carried on my father's shoulders to midnight mass. It was the only time of year when all six

kids got to stay up past eight o'clock. By midnight I'd be so sleepy that everything was like a dream. The music was off in the distance, and the candles were little blobs of light everywhere. The strange shadows on the ceiling scared me, and Dad would hug me tight.

(NELSON *sits down, opens another bag of potato chips and passes it. When it comes to* PEGGY *she speaks to* MRS. BENTLEY.)

PEGGY: I'd like it if you'd sit by me to keep me warm.

MRS. BENTLEY: If you insist. *(She settles next to* PEGGY*)*

BABS: Do you still go to mass?

NELSON: Things change. My father is gone.

BABS: But you could still go.

NELSON: I do. But it isn't the same as my memory. The shadows don't scare me anymore, and the music is out of tune.

MRS. BENTLEY: Humph. You're just growing up.

NELSON: Yes. Now I go to mass because it gives me a comfortable feeling. When I kneel at the altar, I know why.

(They all lapse into silence.)

BABS: Well, Gustav, what's your memory? Oops. Sorry, I just remembered you're Jewish.

GUSTAV: Jewish people have memories, too. My wife and I celebrate Chanukah. We go to the temple. We exchange certain gifts and eat with friends. And we light a candle on the menorah each evening.

BABS: What about a childhood memory?

GUSTAV: *(Reluctantly)* There was a very special Chanukah day. One that can never be equalled.

(GUSTAV *rises and moves to left of center stage, profile to audience, then finally facing audience so the group around the candlelight cannot see his face.)*

NELSON: *(Stage whisper to* PEGGY*)* That's his Hamlet pose.

GUSTAV: When I was seven, the Nazi *(At the word* Nazi *everyone stops eating potato chips and becomes motionless)* soldiers marched into our village and force marched all the Jews to concentration camps. I was playing with a gentile boy in the basement of his house when the soldiers came. The boy's mother hid me for a while, and gradually I appeared in the community as her own. "My boy, Gustav," she would say as she introduced me. She spoke of my family as it would be when they returned. *(Pause)* I prayed for their safe return. Of course, people around the town talked, and as time went on I wept for their deaths. In my own mind I became Gustav Beck instead of Heinle Daniels. That wonderful mother never mentioned my Jewishness. It could have meant death for both of us. But every year at Chanukah she gave me presents. Once a potato when no one had potatoes. Once a red rubber ball. And once each year at Christmas we went to the basement, covered the windows, and she lit the menorah candles. She didn't even know that we light them one each evening. She just lit all of them. And for a few moments I was a Jewish boy.

BABS: What a wonderful gift she gave you.

MRS. BENTLEY: Must you always be center stage, Gustav?

GUSTAV: No. (*Sits on floor, right of* NELSON)

PEGGY: Was that your best Christmas—er—Chanukah gift?

GUSTAV: No.

BABS: What could be better?

GUSTAV: My best gift was not a thing, but a memory. One Christmas night as we prepared to go to the basement, someone pounded on the front door. The mother hugged me to her, and whispered, "The evil Nazis. Don't say a word. Stand next to me, and for God's sake try to act gentile."

PEGGY: Oh!

BABS: My!

GUSTAV: My heart pounded as she opened the door. Suddenly, my sister lifted me off the floor and hugged me until I cried out. When the door slammed shut behind her, she told us that the Nazis had released one female from each building in the camp as a Christmas mockery for Jews. "I may have been followed, so I watch the shadows," my sister said. She told me she would see me again. "Don't give up," she said. Then she was gone. That night when the mother lit all the candles, I said a prayer of thanksgiving for my sister, Mary, the best of all Chanukah gifts.

(GUSTAV *sits lost in thought. Everyone is silent.*)

PEGGY: Did you see her again?

GUSTAV: Not yet.

BABS: Do you think she's still alive?

GUSTAV: Of course! Every year when I light the candles, I *choose* for one more year to believe that some day she will pound on my door. That will be the best of all Chanukah gifts.

BABS:	I felt it when you played the Magi.
GUSTAV:	What?
BABS:	That you knew the terrors of watching the shadows for Herod's soldiers. The fear of discovery became your habit for years. *(Sits in silence a short time)* And in the play, when you argue with yourself about evil and good. You've been there.
GUSTAV:	We are all there!
MRS. BENTLEY:	That was a wonderful story.
BABS:	Will you share a story, Mrs. Bentley?
MRS. BENTLEY:	No.
PEGGY:	Oh, come on.
MRS. BENTLEY:	*(Sharply)* I said no.
BABS:	Come on, Peggy, tell yours.
PEGGY:	I remember decorating the Christmas tree with Susan. I handed her the colored balls, and she hung them.
BABS:	They were all around the bottom.
PEGGY:	And you left them there. And you told us every year it was the prettiest tree we had ever trimmed.
BABS:	It was. And every year you argued over who put on the most tinsel.
PEGGY:	I don't remember that.
BABS:	You did.
PEGGY:	We did?
BABS:	I guess arguing was part of growing up.
NELSON:	I hope that's why we argued all the time. It got on my mom's nerves.
GUSTAV:	*(To* MRS. BENTLEY*)* Did you argue when you were growing up?
MRS. BENTLEY:	No!
GUSTAV:	Come on, everybody argues.
MRS. BENTLEY:	Get it through your head, Gustav Beck, I told you, I have nothing to tell.
	(MRS. BENTLEY jumps up, scattering the cover, and exits stage right. GUSTAV apologizes as she leaves.)
GUSTAV:	I'm sorry. I didn't mean to intrude.

NELSON: Do we know anything about Mrs. Bentley?

GUSTAV: A great deal of her money keeps this theater open between hits.

BABS: Does she have family?

GUSTAV: None that I've heard of.

BABS: Friends?

GUSTAV: She is very aloof. In fact, she's a porcupine, just daring anyone to get close.

NELSON: Sure gets on my case a lot!

PEGGY: Well, I like her.

BABS: She has always treated me fairly. *(Pause)* But she *is* crabby.

GUSTAV: Something in her past makes her unapproachable. My hunch is that she grew up by herself or worse.

NELSON: No family at Christmas?

BABS: It must be a lonely time for her.

PEGGY: Do you think she would spend Christmas with one of us?

BABS: I'll be out of town.

PEGGY: I know.

NELSON: I'll be in Chicago.

GUSTAV: I don't celebrate Christmas.

PEGGY: I do. (PEGGY *goes to the telephone, plugs it in, and listens for the dial tone. She looks up in surprise.)* The phone really is out of order. *(Hurries back under the blanket)* I was going to ask Lucy if I could invite Mrs. Bentley for Christmas.

BABS: Asking an outsider to a family gathering is a lot to ask.

PEGGY: Not now.

BABS: Oh? Why not now?

PEGGY: Lucy told Mrs. Bentley she loved me.

BABS: Is that a new idea to you?

PEGGY: Yes, oh yes. I do think she would agree to invite Mrs. Bentley.

GUSTAV: She may not agree. Don't count on it.

NELSON: Let's all buy Mrs. Bentley a Christmas present. That is, if we ever get out of here to shop for gifts.

PEGGY: I found out a lot about gifts tonight.

GUSTAV:	What's that?
BABS:	What?
PEGGY:	All our childhood Christmas memories were of people, not the gifts we were given. They were gifts without ribbons on boxes.

(MRS. BENTLEY enters stage right, carrying a three-foot artificial Christmas tree. She hesitates in the shadows.)

PEGGY:	*(Not seeing* MRS. BENTLEY*)* I think a Christmas gift is a feeling you give someone at Christmas. *(To* BABS*)* You remembered Grandpa Benedict coming home from the war.
BABS:	You're right.
PEGGY:	*(To* NELSON*)* You remember going to mass with your father. *(To* GUSTAV*)* You remember your sister's promise to return. I'm going to remember Mrs. Bentley eating Christmas dinner with us. Oh, I hope she will come.
MRS. BENTLEY:	*(Steps from the shadows)* I'll come.
PEGGY:	*(Startled, turning around)* You will?
MRS. BENTLEY:	I said I would.
PEGGY:	I'm glad.

(MRS. BENTLEY sits down among the blankets and rugs, placing the Christmas tree in their midst. BABS, NELSON, PEGGY, and GUSTAV voice their approvals with "wonderful, great, pretty tree, good idea.")

MRS. BENTLEY:	*(Sharply)* I'm a grumpy woman with no pretty memories. I have led a gloomy life. But it's time for me to grow up. I stood out there in the prop room feeling sorry for myself and feeling jealous of your Christmas memories.
BABS:	I don't blame you. I'd feel the same way.
MRS. BENTLEY:	No, *you* wouldn't. *(Pause)* I was standing there in the prop room feeling bare and exposed when I saw this little bare Christmas tree. Here I am a fifty-year-old woman pouting in the prop room. For the first time I did something impulsive. I grabbed the bare tree. Let's make a memory.
BABS:	*(Reaches for* MRS. BENTLEY's *hand)* You're wonderful.
MRS. BENTLEY:	*(Pulls her hand away, speaks in her old sarcastic tone)* I brought the scissors.
GUSTAV:	For what?

(MRS. BENTLEY reaches for a potato chip wrapper, which she shreds into tree tinsel. She hands some shreds to GUSTAV *and* PEGGY, *then cuts more.)*

NELSON: Here, put more on this side.

PEGGY: When we finish, we can argue over who put on the most potato chip wrapper tinsel.

(Everyone laughs and throws more tinsel on the tree.)

DISCUSSION QUESTIONS

The play needs no discussion in order for your event to be complete. If, however, you wish to discuss, choose your emphasis: (1) dealing with a blended family, (2) honesty in Christmas gifts, or (3) helping the lonely at Christmas.

Dealing with a Blended Family

1. Peggy has experienced divorce. How do you think she felt and is feeling? (Consider that divorce brings grief that must be worked through. When divorce involves remarriage of a parent, adjustment to new family is heaped on top of grief.)
2. Do you think that, as Peggy said, divorced kids have to hide their feelings and talk a certain way? How? What walls does this build between people? As years go by, does hiding feelings and talking a certain way make people grow apart or together?
3. The rhythm and comfort of our lives is something based on rituals. (Explain rituals to children as something done repeatedly until it becomes the expected thing, such as going out together for hamburgers every Friday night, celebrating Christmas a certain way, and going to church together.) What rituals change or disappear when a divorce occurs? How can we build new rituals to add stability to our lives? Why do we put off doing that? (Sometimes the fear that we will forget the emotion of past rituals makes us shrink from building new ones, or we fear that the new ones will be snatched away just as the old ones were.)
4. How might a person feel about having the court or the judge tell him or her how to celebrate holidays?
5. What other problems arise for divorced persons during holidays? How can the church help ease these problems through its extended family?
6. Draw a picture of your favorite childhood memory. Share it with the group. Or draw a picture of one of the memories of a character in the play. What questions occurred to you as you drew?

Honesty in Christmas Gifts

1. What is a gift?
2. Do you agree that "a gift makes a statement about the giver"? Why? Why not?

3. Had you ever considered that the wise men who went home without telling the whereabouts of Jesus gave him a gift? Many gifts go unnoticed. Review the past week in your mind. What gifts were given to you? What gifts did you give?

4. What does your Christmas gift-giving list reflect? Is it a pleasure to give the gifts? Are you the designated gift buyer in your family? If so, how does this affect the way you feel about buying the designated gifts? Is it idealistic to think that every person should buy his or her own gifts?

5. Discuss alternatives to gift buying.

6. How can gift giving, a symbolic Christmas tradition, camouflage the real celebration of Christmas?

7. What is an honest gift?

Helping the Lonely at Christmas

1. In the play, Mrs. Bentley was lonely. Do you think she was lonely every day or just on Christmas? Do we have to know why she was lonely in order to want to befriend her?

2. What is required of anyone who wants to help lonely persons at Christmas? At any time of the year?

3. Who comes to your mind when we say "the lonely"? A group of persons? Penitentiary inmates? Persons hospitalized or in nursing homes? Travelers? Neighbors?

4. How can one extend a hand or throw a blanket of love around a lonely person?

5. How do gifts (of all kinds) help a lonely person?

EVENT THEME: CELEBRATE GOD!

SCHEDULE

*Get nametags.
*Get Together Activity:
1. Have guided tours of your place of worship.
2. Have dinner or refreshments and singing. Include "Sing This Song and Celebrate."
*Focus Activity:
1. Perform playlet, "Early Dawn Worship" or
2. Optional skit, "Sunday Morning Whispers."
*Sharing Time:
1. Plan a secret worship service or
2. In groups, discuss celebration.
*Closing:
1. Instruct groups to hold secret services.
2. Optional singing or Reader's Theater, "Wind, Fire, Sparks."

ADVANCE PREPARATION

*Recruit a moderator.
*Recruit a song leader and make copies of music.
*Recruit a drama director.
*Select and instruct guides for tours of sanctuary. Your church may have more than one area of worship. Decide what you will include in the tour. If your event includes young children, plan time for them to touch the organ, candles, hearing outlets for the deaf, try out the pulpit, and so forth. Include the following in the tour: The history of the sanctuary, the view from the choir loft, reasons for kneeling at the altar, and significant symbolism.
*If you plan discussion as a part of this event, recruit and instruct leaders.
*Designate responsibility for nametags.

ROOM ARRANGEMENT

*For "Early Dawn Worship A.D. 112," arrange chairs around an open area forming a theater-in-the-round. Make an aisle on each side for passage of actors to drama area.

*For "Sunday Morning Whispers," arrange chairs in front of a staging area that is backed to a wall. Place sound equipment at back of the room.

AS PEOPLE ARRIVE

*Get nametags. If you have a large group, designate groups to leave for tours every ten minutes. For smaller groups, assemble and go to the sanctuary together.

FOCUS ACTIVITY

EARLY DAWN WORSHIP A.D. 112

A playlet.

Production Notes

Characters: Narrator; Proto (the assertive leader), tall male adult; Daniel, (his nervous, short-tempered friend), shorter male adult; Elizabeth (forty-to fifty-year-old) female; her teenage son Philip; a very old couple, Anna and Thomas; and Trunner, adult male. Designate one of these characters to lead the singing in the playlet.

Playing time: 10 minutes.

Properties: Three torches, a large, deep container of sand. Option: Use lanterns or lamps and provide a rock or cube to set them on. They are the only stage light; arrange them high enough to illuminate the actors' faces.

Sound: A tape recording of soldiers marching.

Costumes: Women wear basic ankle length garments with a hole cut out for the head, and hooded cloaks made by folding a two- or three-yard strip of material with wrong sides together. Make a seam at one end and reverse the garment so material is right side out. The seam forms a hood, and the rest of the material is wound around the shoulders. Men wear a belted shorter version of the flat garment with loosely fitting pants. Men and women wear sandals.

Setting: Create a night hillside effect with what you have on hand, or play the scene on a bare stage.

NARRATOR: In A.D. 112 Pliny the Younger, governor of Bithynia, wrote a letter to Emperor Trajan in which he described his view of Christian worship. The letter gives us details about one of the many groups of Christians who met before dawn to sing and bind themselves with oaths. Since that time there have been many changes in the way we dress and eat and conduct our business. Even our places of worship have changed, but our basic reasons for getting together as Christians have remained the same.

Listen for these reasons as we meet Proto and Daniel, part of the second-century underground.

(The stage is dark and empty except for the bucket of sand, stage center. PROTO *enters stage left carrying a lighted torch. At center stage he plants the torch in the container of sand, inspects the area for intruders, and returns to the torch.* DANIEL *enters stage right also carrying a lighted torch.* PROTO *turns to meet* DANIEL *as he sees the light)*

PROTO: Greetings. Peace be to you.

DANIEL: And to you. *(Plants the torch and stands to the right of it.)*

PROTO: You're very good.

DANIEL: Good?

PROTO: At quietly appearing from nowhere.

DANIEL: The alternative is . . . is deadly.

PROTO: Were you seen leaving your house?

DANIEL: Who knows?

PROTO: But you were careful?

DANIEL: *(Snorts in disgust)* Of *course* I was careful. Do you take me for a fool? You're the one who just said I was good!

PROTO: No need to be irritable.

DANIEL: Oh. *(Apologetically)* Sorry. I'm very edgy these days. *(Pause)* Life as a Christian is dangerous. It's not easy to live up to the vows without being noticed.

PROTO: But you're usually a patient man. You can do it.

DANIEL: *(Moves around glancing into the shadows)* It's easier for you.

PROTO: How's that?

DANIEL: With your position in Pliny's palace, no one suspects you of being a Christian.

PROTO: Still, I'm careful.

DANIEL: But trusted in the palace. What goes on there these days?

PROTO: There's good news and bad news.

DANIEL: *(Impatiently, standing hunched)* Well?

PROTO: The good news is a letter to Pliny from Emperor Trajan. The emperor tells Pliny that Christians are no longer to be hunted down like animals.

DANIEL: A weight has been lifted from my shoulders. *(Stands taller)*

PROTO: Wait! The bad news is that if someone is discovered to be Christian, he or she will be given the *opportunity* to renounce the faith. *(Pause)* Anyone who refuses will be executed.

DANIEL: *(Groans)* We're back to fear again. *(Paces back and forth, obviously agitated)*

PROTO: God will take care of us in his way.

DANIEL: Tell that to the dead ones.

PROTO: But God will take care of us.

DANIEL: I believe it, but I'm still all nerves. I worry. *(Holds hand toward the torch for warming)* Where is everyone? Where's Elizabeth?

PROTO: No one has seen her for two days.

DANIEL: *(In anguish)* Oh, no! And Thomas and Anna?

PROTO: They are waiting for the late patrol to pass their house. *(Pause)* And the Jacobs family is sick with fever.

DANIEL: Well then, where's Rachael?

PROTO: Rachael and her children aren't coming. Her house has been watched since they executed her husband.

DANIEL: Is this meeting really worth risking our lives for? *(Looks around in the shadows)*

PROTO: Don't falter, Daniel. The meeting is a worship celebration. And it's a commitment to God.

DANIEL: I know what it is, but I wonder if we couldn't commit to God alone at home with less risk. I'm told that Jesus went apart to be alone.

PROTO: True, but we need contact with people who truly worship and who vow themselves to God. Don't giving thanks and singing make you feel less fearful?

DANIEL: Yes.

PROTO: And, don't you get strength from the other believers?

DANIEL: *(Affirmative nod in silence)* Where are they?

PROTO: They'll be here before daybreak.

DANIEL: Shh. Listen.

(From stage left comes the distant sounds of two marching soldiers.)

PROTO: Come close to the torch and make it known that we're visiting.

(They move close and stand motionless as the footsteps recede.)

DANIEL:	Will they come back?
PROTO:	No. They have a five mile radius to cover before dawn.

(ELIZABETH, PHILIP, ANNA, and THOMAS step out of the shadows of stage left. They enter the circle of light and hug and kiss each other during the conversation.)

PROTO:	*(Hugging ANNA and THOMAS)* Peace be to you.
ANNA:	And you.
THOMAS:	And to you.
DANIEL:	Peace to you, Elizabeth.
ELIZABETH:	The soldiers were late tonight.
PROTO:	*(Laughing)* Christians are patient.
PHILIP:	Where's Trunner?

(They look around in silence, realizing that he is not there.)

PHILIP:	Shall we wait?
PROTO:	No. Even in trial we live in the Lord. The Lord bless Trunner. We must begin now, or daylight will betray us as we go home.

(They begin singing "Sing This Song and Celebrate" as they form a circle around the light. Music for this chorus is found on pg. 53.)

> Sing this song and celebrate
>   the life that God has given you!
> Praise the Lord, and celebrate
>   with joy forever new.

DANIEL:	We have been taught to sing and make music in our hearts unto the Lord. We give thanks to God the Father for everything.
ALL TOGETHER:	In the name of our Lord Jesus Christ. *(Raising their arms, palms toward the light, the group becomes very joyful, and slightly sways to the music as they sing the chorus again. During the singing TRUNNER enters stage right carrying a light. An opening is made for him to join the circle. He places his light in the center with the other torches, nods to each one establishing eye contact, and takes his place in the circle as everyone continues singing.)*

> Sing the song and celebrate
>   the life that God has given you.
> Praise the Lord and celebrate
>   with joy forever new.

TRUNNER:	Peace be to you.

ALL TOGETHER:	*(Not in unison)* And you.
PHILIP:	I have learned the scripture from Isaiah from my grandfather.
PROTO:	It's good that a young person is learning the scriptures. Will you say it?
PHILIP:	Grandfather said this passage was one used by our Lord Jesus. "The spirit of the Lord is on me, because the Lord has anointed me to preach the good news to the poor. He has sent me to proclaim freedom for the prisoners and recovery of sight for the blind [and] to release the oppressed" (Luke 4:18).
PROTO:	Our Lord Jesus did those things.
ALL TOGETHER:	*(With hands up, palms toward light)* We are thankful.
PROTO:	The peace of Christ rules in our hearts as members of one body.
ALL TOGETHER:	*(Hands up, palms toward the light)* We are thankful.
PROTO:	Our Lord taught us of the love that binds us together in perfect unity.
ALL TOGETHER:	*(Hands up, palms toward the light)* We are thankful.
PROTO:	Our Lord taught us to share that love with the hungry, the stranger, the naked, and the prisoner.
ALL TOGETHER:	We are thankful.
PROTO:	Jesus died for our sins and promises forgiveness.
ALL TOGETHER:	*(Hands up, clap)* We are thankful. *(Take hands down)*
PROTO:	*(PROTO nods to ELIZABETH)* Elizabeth, will you lead the vows this time?
ELIZABETH:	Yes. Our attitude should be the same as that of our Lord Jesus Christ. Lord, we promise to take on the nature of a servant of God. Let's say the agreed vows.
ALL TOGETHER:	We promise to put on the whole armor of God, to stand firm with the belt of truth buckled about our waists, so that we may live wisely. We will devote ourselves to prayer.

We will be wise with outsiders, making the most of every opportunity.
We will not get drunk or commit any wicked deed.
We will abstain from fraud, theft, and adultery.
Lord, we will never break our word or deny a trust when called upon to honor it.
We will try to understand God's will.
We will forgive as God forgives us.
Silently we say the names of those we forgive. *(Pause)*
Lord, We silently ask you to forgive our sins and take the weight of them from us. *(Pause)*

PROTO: *(In stage whisper to* TRUNNER*)* It's nearing daylight. Go watch for the soldiers.

TRUNNER: *(In stage whisper)* Yes. *(Moves to stage left, looking to distance)*

ALL TOGETHER: *(Continuing as before)* Whatever happens, we promise to conduct ourselves in a manner worthy of the good news of Christ.

TRUNNER: *(Moves quickly to the circle)* The soldiers are coming! Meet at my house for the morning meal.

(Whispers of "peace, peace" are heard as PROTO *douses the lights in the sand and one by one everyone fades into the darkness as the sound of marching soldiers is heard in the distance. The house lights remain off for five seconds after the soldiers retreat into the distance.)*

SHARING TIME

The moderator may elect to close with everyone singing "Sing This Song and Celebrate" (pg. 53) or continue with discussion questions.
For a group that includes young children:

1. According to the drama, why did the early Christians get together?
2. If you had only a few minutes in which to celebrate with other Christians, what would you do? Plan and carry out in your own group a celebration meeting. This must be spontaneous, simple, and straight from the heart; no Bibles, props, or crosses. Let the *children* help do this! They have a way of breaking ideas down to essentials. Note: If your group finds this stimulating, perhaps they would like to plan another secluded worship event.

For a group with older children, youth, and adults—or if you prefer discussion:

1. Why did these early Christians meet? Why did they meet in a field instead of a home?

2. What did it cost to be a Christian in the second century?
3. The early Christians had to trim their worship celebration down to the essentials. What were the essentials? (Suggestions: Putting oneself under the control of God, group love and fellowship, thanksgiving, celebrating joy in the Lord, giving and receiving forgiveness, reminding themselves through vows how they wanted to act. By taking on the nature of a servant, the early Christians also worshiped God in their daily lives by being the hands and feet of God's love to the hungry and oppressed.)
4. This playlet used many scriptures. Read each one and discuss with this question in mind: How will I carry this out in my daily life this week? See Ephesians 5:19-20, 6:10; Isaiah 60:1 (also found in Luke 4:16, Matthew 11:5); Colossians 3:12-17, 4:2-6; and Philippians 1:27, 2:5-7.
5. Close the discussion in a circle, reading the vows from the playlet that you have copied. Sing the chorus of "Sing This Song and Celebrate."

ALTERNATE ACTIVITY

SUNDAY MORNING WHISPERS
A small boy asks questions and sees a mouse during worship.

Production Notes

Characters: Moderator; Jere, a young boy; Julie, his sister; Mom; Mr. Swift, an older man; Minister, an offstage voice; Mouse Puller, a male or female, any age, who hides under the table and pulls the toy mouse.

Playing time: 5 minutes.

Properties: Rows of folding chairs, a purse for Mom with a small book in it, a table with a long table cloth, a cross, two candles, a toy mouse attached to wire or string, and recorded music.

Sound effects: Prerecorded congregational singing of last verse of "Stand Up and Bless the Lord" (United Methodist Hymnal, pg. 662). Recruit an operator for the cassette player.

Costumes: Sunday church clothes.

Setting: Sunday morning worship with five rows of folding chairs lined up diagonally on stage. Downstage left, facing the rows of chairs, is a worship center table covered by a long tablecloth, with a cross and two candlesticks with burning candles. The mandatory cloth on the table hides the person pulling the string on the mouse. Mr. Swift sits downstage right in a chair on the end of the fifth row. On the row in front of him (fourth row) sit Jere (nearest the audience), Mom (in the second chair), and Julie (in the third chair). At the end of the fourth row, downstage, is a toy mouse attached to a wire or string that is pulled toward the worship table by Mouse Puller, who is concealed by the table cloth.

MODERATOR: The Celebration Players have invited us to join us for last Sunday's worship service. Julie and Jere, whose father sings in the choir, sit with their mother toward the back of the sanctuary. A church friend, Mr. Swift, sits behind them.

(JERE, MOM, JULIE, and MR. SWIFT *enter, stage right and stand in front of their chairs. Recorded music of third verse of "Stand Up and Bless the Lord" fades in and continues to Amen. They sit down as the music ends.)*

JULIE: *(In stage whisper to* MOM*)* Why do we always come to church?

MOM: To worship and to learn.

JULIE: What's worship?

MOM: Shhh. *(Stage whisper)* To celebrate God, or oh, lots of things. I'll explain later.

JERE: *(Pointing to candles)* Why do we always have candles?

MOM: They remind us that Jesus was the light of the world.

MR. SWIFT: (MR. SWIFT *taps* JERE *on the shoulder and speaks softly)* They also stand for the Holy Spirit.

JERE: *(Loudly)* What's that?

MOM: Shhh.

MR. SWIFT: I'll tell you after church.

                  (MR. SWIFT *sits back and* JERE *again faces the front. They sit in silence a few seconds.)*

JERE: *(Pointing to the cross)* You told me about the cross last week.

MR. SWIFT: Shhh.

JERE: *(Learning toward* MOM*)* What I want to know is, did Jesus really live?

JULIE: Of course, silly. *(Shuffles her feet and squirms in her seat)*

MOM: The Bible tells about him. Other men who lived at that time later wrote about him.

JERE: Did he go to church like me?

                  (JULIE *fidgets. While* MOM *is talking, she takes a small book from her purse and hands it to* JULIE.*)*

MOM: He went to a synagogue, not quite like our church.

JERE: I believe in Jesus. I just wanted to know.

                  (MR. SWIFT *taps* JERE *on the shoulder.* JERE *turns around and looks as* MR. SWIFT *says shh with his fingers in front of his mouth.)*

MINISTER:	*(Offstage)* I say to you, to celebrate God is to celebrate the people around you. And to celebrate God means to put yourself under the control of God. Celebrating puts you in touch with the mystery of the spiritual in the universe. Celebrating God is to say yes to him and feel joyful. When a person truly celebrates God, the answers to life's questions become apparent to him.
	(The toy mouse begins to move very slowly toward the worship center.)
JERE:	*(Loud stage whisper)* Mom!
MOM:	Shh.
JERE:	Mom! Mom!
MOM:	Shhh.
JULIE:	Eeek.
JERE:	May I keep him?
MOM:	Who?
JERE:	If I catch the mouse, may I keep him?
MOM:	What mouse?
JERE:	*(Pointing to mouse)* That mouse.
	(MOM quickly pulls her feet up. JULIE sits on her feet. JERE starts out of his chair to go for the mouse, but MR. SWIFT places a firm right hand on JERE's shoulder, holding him in the chair. The mouse quickly moves out of sight under the worship table.)
MINISTER:	*(Voice offstage, left)* In conclusion, I remind you that we are called upon in our journey in faith to celebrate God. *(Pause)* Please stand for the benediction.
	(JERE, MOM, JULIE, and MR. SWIFT stand.)
JERE:	Why do we stand up now and not all the time?
MOM:	Shh.
JERE:	Can we celebrate without standing up?
MR. SWIFT:	Shh. Yes.
JERE:	*(Turning to MR. SWIFT)* How?
MR. SWIFT:	Celebration is in the heart—a gladness inside you.
JERE:	Yeah. I do that. *(He sits down and tugs at MOM's arm.)*
MOM:	Shh. Be quiet. This is a prayer.
JERE:	But it's an important question.

MOM: What?

JERE: Are we going to McDonald's for lunch?

Moderator leads applause for the Celebration Players as the mouse puller and minister step onstage.

Some churches give young churchgoers coloring packets. Others plan a junior church service. Others welcome children in the service of worship and tolerate their squirms and questions as part of the learning process. Know your congregation as you plan the event's next step.

IF YOU CHOOSE SMALL GROUP DISCUSSION:

Questions move from concrete to abstract. Use the first few questions with groups having young children. Select questions to fit your needs.

1. Who was your favorite character in the skit? Why?
2. Have you ever seen a mouse in church? (The author's sanctuary has been visited by birds, and once a lizard crawled down her row to the delight of her children.) What are other distractions in worship?
3. Where do you like to sit in church? Why?
4. A worshiping congregation is made up of loving people. Whom do you notice first thing after sitting down?
5. What do you do during church? (Intergenerational sharing of answers is especially important.)
6. If you think of questions during church, how can you get those questions answered? (Note taking can be important for all ages, especially for parents who are asked verbal questions during worship.)
7. How do you feel during worship in the sanctuary? People can celebrate God any time and any place, but there is something special about worshiping with others. Do you feel that way at any other time or location? Since the time of early secret worship services, the Christian church is said to "have altar—will travel." The act or feeling of worship may occur any place. For some, an act of worship is also a role of social servant—feeding the hungry, housing the homeless, and so forth.

Going a little deeper:
8. What are symbols in your place of worship, and how can they help you focus your attention on God?
9. How did the skit define worship? (Celebrating God, celebrating the people around you, putting yourself under the control of God, getting in touch with the spirit of God and allowing the Holy Spirit to enter your life, journey in faith as a way of worshiping God.) Add your ideas to those definitions.
10. How did Jesus celebrate God in his lifetime?
11. How can you celebrate God?

CLOSING

Sing the song "Sing This Song and Celebrate," p. 53, or use Reader's Theater.

Reader's Theater

This reading drama uses three groups of four readers to achieve the effect of wind, fire, and sparks moving across those assembled. Play with the acoustics of your performance room, and orchestrate the voices to gather momentum and volume by the end of the presentation.

WIND, FIRE, SPARKS

Setting: Wind voices 1, 2, 3, and 4 stand to the left and in front of the intergenerational group. Fire voices 1, 2, 3, and 4 stand to the right and front of the group. Sparks voices 1, 2, 3, and 4 stand in back of the group, facing the front. Rehearse readers in the performance room. The rhythm of reading should be slow enough to be understood, but gather momentum in appropriate places.

Turn the lights low, and ask intergenerational participants to close their eyes for the drama "Wind, Fire, Sparks."

WIND VOICE 1: *(Softly)* Wind.

WIND VOICE 2: *(Less softly)* Wind,

WIND VOICE 3: *(Louder)* Wind!

WIND VOICE 4: Hear the whisper of the wind:

WIND VOICE 1: *(Stage whisper)* God

WIND VOICE 2: *(Stage whisper)* is

WIND VOICE 3: *(A little louder)* love!

WIND VOICE 1: *(Louder stage whisper)* God

WIND VOICE 2: *(Louder stage whisper)* is

WIND VOICE 3: *(Still louder stage whisper)* love!

WIND VOICE 1: *(Softly)* Wind,

WIND VOICE 2: *(Louder)* Wind,

WIND VOICE 3: *(Loudly)* Wind.

WIND VOICE 4: Feel God's love blowing

WIND VOICE 1: among us.

WIND VOICE 2: *(Softly)* Wind.

WIND VOICE 3: *(Fading)* Wind.

FIRE VOICE 1:   *(Simply stated, moderately loud)* Fire.

FIRE VOICE 2:   *(Loudly)* Fire,

FIRE VOICE 3:   *(Louder)* Fire!

FIRE VOICE 4:   Burning spirit:

FIRE VOICE 1:   Love

FIRE VOICE 2:   one

FIRE VOICE 3:   *(Evenly, moderately loud)* another.

FIRE VOICE 1:   Love

FIRE VOICE 2:   one

FIRE VOICE 3:   *(Evenly, moderately loud)* another.

FIRE VOICE 1:   *(Loudly)* Fire.

FIRE VOICE 2:   *(Softer)* Fire,

FIRE VOICE 3:   *(Softer)* Fire!

FIRE VOICE 4:   Warming our circle

FIRE VOICE 1:   *(softly)* Wind

FIRE VOICE 2:   *(Louder)* Scattering

FIRE VOICE 3:   *(Loudly)* Sparks!

SPARKS VOICE 1:   *(Softly)* Sparks.

SPARKS VOICE 2:   *(Louder)* Sparks,

SPARKS VOICE 3:   *(Loudly)* Sparks!

SPARKS VOICE 4:   Whispers fanning to the broken and needy:

SPARKS VOICE 1:   *(Stage whisper)* We

SPARKS VOICE 2:   *(Stage whisper)* love

SPARKS VOICE 3:   *(Stage whisper)* you.

SPARKS VOICE 1:   *(Louder)* We

SPARKS VOICE 2:   *(Louder)* love

SPARKS VOICE 3:   *(Louder still)* you!

SPARKS VOICE 1:   *(Loudly)* Sparks.

SPARKS VOICE 2:   *(Softly)* Sparks,

SPARKS VOICE 3:   *(Softer)* Sparks!

SPARKS VOICE 4,
FIRE VOICE 4,
WIND VOICE 4:   We celebrate God with

SPARKS VOICE 1,
WIND VOICE 1:   *(Softly)* Wind!

SPARKS VOICE 1,
FIRE VOICE 1,
WIND VOICE 1:   *(Louder)* Fire!

SPARKS VOICE 1,
FIRE VOICE 1,
WIND VOICE 1,
SPARKS VOICE 4:   *(Louder)* And sparks!

EVENT THEME: GAME NIGHT (OR DAY)

A GET ACQUAINTED AND PLAY TOGETHER TIME

SCHEDULE

*Get nametags.
*Get Together Activities:
  1. Make Heart Family headbands.
  2. Distribute individual score sheets.
*Focus Activity:
  1. (Small group) Play games together.
  2. (Large group) Heart Families circulate to game groups.
  3. Play Speechless Team Charade.
  4. Tally scores.
  5. Have a prize presentation.
*Closing time:
  1. Have a circle of winners.
  2. Serve refreshments.

ADVANCE PREPARATION

*Select the type of game night you wish to have. Use the group games suggested here, or set up board games at cardtables and/or Ping Pong, shuffleboard, and so forth. If your group is small, play get acquainted games and other circle games without keeping score. Divide a larger group into smaller units, keeping Heart Family groups together. Heart Family is an adoption program for pairing single children, youth, or adults with a family unit. Plan for persons with handicapping conditions. Include some uncomplicated games for persons with limited mental capacity, and plan assistance for those with physical limitations.
*Recruit a chairperson for the event.
*Select and instruct game leaders.
*Make and copy score sheets. Some games have actual scores, others are not competitive for scores. Give each participant ten points.

*Recruit director for making Heart Family headbands and collect supplies. Keep it simple: strips of felt, paper, rope, torn cloth strips of various colors and prints, and paper sacks that can be cut into strips and decorated.

ROOM ARRANGEMENT

*A table for nametags.
*Tables for making headbands.
*Tables and/or chairs according to chosen game plan.

AS PEOPLE ARRIVE

*Get nametags.
*Make Heart Family headbands.
*Distribute score sheets and pencils if you plan to use them.

FOCUS ACTIVITIES

Family Circle

Goal: Get the most bodies inside a marked circle. Bonus points are given for learning the first names of those in the circle. You will need:

1. A referee who can count.
2. Four-foot masking tape circles on the floor.
3. A pre-set time limit.

Hand Decorating Contest

Goal: Let someone decorate your hand with paper, stickers, glitter, nail polish, water paint, and/or washable markers. You will need:

1. A supervisor.
2. *Pre-tested* supplies.

Paper Airplane Contest

Goal: With someone else, make and decorate a paper airplane, and/or fly it in a distance contest. You will need:

1. An instructor.
2. Paper, crayons, scissors, markers, pens, paper clips, and transparent tape on a table.
3. A corridor free of pedestrian traffic that has been marked off in increments of five feet.
4. A judge in that corridor.

I Wish I Were A . . .

Goal: Be the last person in a circle of echo pantomime. You will need:

1. A leader to explain the game.
2. A standing circle of twelve to fifteen players of all ages.

This is an echo pantomime where the leader says, "I wish I were a (fill in the blank) lion," and acts out a lion. Players echo, "I wish I were a lion," and pantomime a lion. Next players says, "I wish I were a (first grader or anything)," and pantomimes the lion followed by his pantomime of what a first grader does. The group echoes the wishes and pantomimes the actions. Play continues with each player adding his or her own wish, but always echoing and pantomiming the previous wishes. A player who cannot echo and pantomime all the previous wishes is out of the game.

Domino Fall

Goal: In cooperation with your Heart Family, set up a domino design. Collect a crowd to watch it fall. You will need:

1. Printed instructions on a sign or an instructor to designate the basic designs from which a group may choose, such as dove of peace, intertwined hearts, a stained-glass illustration in your church, a birthday cake, or map of your state.
2. As many dominoes as you can collect.
3. A roped-off area for the set up. Instead of the floor, for the convenience of participants, you may need to use tables pushed together.

Old MacDonald*

Sing "Old MacDonald Had a Farm," but substitute the name and action, hobby, favorite sound, or favorite food of each person in the group. For example, "Old MacDonald had a farm, and on that farm he had a Charles . . . With a baseball here and a baseball there," and so forth. Try to fit the name to a hobby or positive personal characteristic. Do each person in the group.

Theme and Throw*

You will need: Chairs and a ball.
Players stand or sit in a circle. The leader mentions a particular item or concept while throwing the ball to a player. The ball is then passed around,

*Old MacDonald and Theme and Throw are from *New Games for Community,* Christine Gapes, Board of Education Uniting Church NSU, Sidney, Australia, 1978.

and each person who throws it must say something within that theme. For example: Theme—Ice Cream. Throw—strawberry, cone, cold, or chocolate. Theme—School. Throw—pencil, books, or chalkboards.

SPEECHLESS TEAM CHARADE

Goal: To challenge the imagination. Enjoy laughing. Develop group cooperation.

You will need: A time keeper, a stopwatch, chalkboard or large paper for keeping score, a box filled with papers on which you have written charades to be acted out (farm, shoe factory, church, school, Peace Corps, baseball team, hot air balloon team, Burger King kitchen, Baskin-Robbins, garbage collection, circus parade, game show).

Divide into two groups.

Appoint a leader in each group. Have the leader draw a slip of paper with an action or item written on it that he or she interprets *quietly* to his or her group. Have the group plan their charade for the other group using everyone on the team.

The guessing team must confer and give the team leader a guess to be presented to the game leader. Write down the time it took the guessers to get the correct answer. Set a three-minute maximum time limit. At game's end, the group with the *smallest* score wins. If the opposing team does not guess the charade, subtract ten points from the actors' team score.

CLOSING

Gather in a circle. Moderator will recap fun of the evening and present a prize to the highest scorer or highest Heart Family unit score.

Say something along these lines: Tonight we have celebrated our church family with joy and fun.

In the game of dominoes we are all doubles.
In the checkerboard of life we are all crowned.
In baseball, we are all World Series winners.
In the game of Speechless Team Charade we are all winning teams.
In the big Monopoly game of life, we are all Park Place.
Because of the special feelings we have for each other in our church family, and because God loves us, we are all special, all winners.
Squeeze a winner's hand and say goodbye.

INDEX